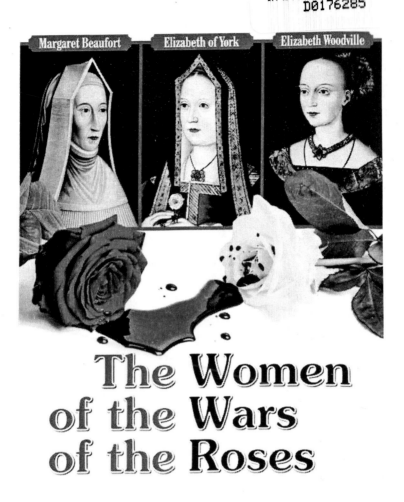

Margaret Beaufort   Elizabeth of York   Elizabeth Woodville

The Women of the Wars of the Roses

Alicia Carter

ISBN-13: 978-1491280096

ISBN-10: 1491280093

Table of Contents

Prologue 1

Glossary of names 5

PART ONE: Elizabeth Woodville 10

1.   What did Elizabeth Woodville look like? 12

2.   The Woodvilles, a family raised high 22

3.   Elizabeth, witchcraft charges and the legendary Melusine 48

4.   Elizabeth's reputation: The haughty, vengeful, greedy Queen? 64

5.   Elizabeth, the Princes in the Tower and Richard III 78

PART TWO: Margaret Beaufort 88

6.   The richest heiress in England 90

7.   What did Margaret look like? 110

8.   Margaret Beaufort and the plots of 1483 114

9.   Was Margaret Beaufort a "mother-in-law from hell"? 122

PART THREE: Elizabeth of York 134

10.   The true heiress of the House of York 136

11.   Was Elizabeth Richard III's lover? 146

12.   Elizabeth's marriage to Henry Tudor—what was it like? 158

13. What did Elizabeth of York spend her money on? 172

Epilogue: The three survivors and their legacy 182

Bibliography 196

Prologue

In August 1485, when Henry VII won the Battle of Bosworth, killing Richard III and putting an end to a Yorkist regime, no one could predict that the Tudor dynasty would stay on the throne of England for more than a century. Margaret Beaufort, Henry VII's mother, wept during her only son's coronation, but they were not the tears of joy. Her confessor, John Fisher, would later say that she was afraid that an adversity was lurking behind every triumph. She, of all women, would know that being King during the turbulent period of civil unrest was a very dangerous business.

Unlike his predecessors, who were either murdered within the Tower of London, like the Lancastrian King Henry VI, or killed in a battle for the crown, like Richard III, Henry VII managed to stay on the throne and pass his claim to his son. His marriage to the Yorkist heiress, Elizabeth of York, proved both fertile and successful. Among the children born out of this union was the future Henry VIII—the King who casts a large shadow over his parents.

Reared on the memory of the Wars of the Roses, Henry VIII had been taught to believe that without a male heir, those wars could break out again. Henry himself was a "spare heir"—a second son, not destined to rule but to take the place in the succession in case of the death of his elder brother, Arthur. Shortly after his brother's death in 1502, Prince Henry became the most precious boy in the whole of England—he was heir to the throne, the only remaining son of Henry VII. Elizabeth of York bore three sons, but two of them died, leaving young Henry the only hope of the newly founded dynasty. Elizabeth herself died in early 1503, after she had prematurely given birth to a daughter. Without his Queen and without his eldest son, in whom he had put his hopes, Henry VII was left with a boy who would, eventually, become the icon of the Tudor dynasty.

To understand Henry VIII's fanatical obsession to leave a male heir to the throne, one must understand the "Wars of the Roses". At the time, the conflict was known as "the Cousins' War", acknowledging that it was a family feud. The two families—Lancaster and York—fought for the throne of England between 1455 and 1485. Although this war was fought mainly by men on the battlefield, it was not only the work of ambitious men. Three women emerged as the ultimate survivors of this bloody conflict: Elizabeth

Woodville, Margaret Beaufort and Elizabeth of York. This book tells their story.

These women have one thing in common: they helped to shape the early Tudor dynasty. Elizabeth Woodville, a Lancastrian widow turned Yorkist Queen, was the first commoner to marry the King of England. Margaret Beaufort was only a child of thirteen when she gave birth to the future King Henry VII of England, although neither she nor her son could possibly know what the future held for them. Elizabeth of York, Henry VII's wife, was a daughter of Elizabeth Woodville and she was the first Tudor Queen consort, but she is often merely a footnote in history.

The purpose of this book is to retrieve Elizabeth Woodville, Margaret Beaufort and Elizabeth of York from obscurity and bring these real, thinking individuals to you, dear Reader. Although there is much space and emphasis given to the times these women lived in, the strongest emphasis is on their lives and the choices they had to make to survive the Wars of the Roses.

To hear these women, and to understand them, it is necessary to disentangle the many myths surrounding them. This book concentrates on dispelling some of the most enduring myths about Elizabeth Woodville, Margaret

3

Beaufort and Elizabeth of York, bringing these women back to life. The England during the Wars of the Roses was a world of violence, superstition and uncertainty—and the women who feature in this book had to wade through all of that in order to emerge victorious. Let me plunge you into this world and show you what experiences shaped these women's characters and allowed them to become what they are to us today—the epitome of perseverance and strength.

Glossary of names

The Kings of England (1464-1485):

Henry VI: The Lancastrian King, deposed twice. His mental collapse and inadequacy in ruling the country led to the wars for succession. He was murdered within the Tower of London in May 1471.

Edward IV: The Yorkist King, Son of Richard, Duke of York, who fought for the throne. His father was killed during the Battle of Wakefield in 1460, but Edward would eventually win the crown. Briefly deposed in 1470, he quickly recovered his kingdom. He died in April 1483.

Edward V: Edward IV's son and heir. He was twelve at the time of his father's death and was never crowned. Deposed and send to the Tower, his fate remains unknown.

Richard III: Edward IV's brother and the last Yorkist King. He deposed and disinherited his nephews. He was killed at the Battle of Bosworth Field in August 1485.

Henry VII: Founder of the Tudor dynasty, he won the crown by conquest. He married Edward IV's eldest daughter, Elizabeth of York, and begat several children by her. Henry died of tuberculosis in April 1509.

The Queens of England (1464-1485)

Marguerite of Anjou: Born in France as a daughter of René of Anjou, King of Naples, she was fifteen at the time of her marriage to Henry VI in 1445 and for many years was unable to conceive a child. This finally changed in 1453 when she gave birth to her only son, Edward of Westminster. Marguerite was highly unpopular in England because she wanted to be regent for her son and fought for his rights until the boy's death in 1471. Marguerite died in 1482.

Elizabeth Woodville: The first English Queen consort since the eleventh century, Elizabeth was a daughter of a knight and a European duchess. She first married John Grey and bore him two sons. John Grey was killed while leading the Lancastrian cavalry during the Second Battle of St Albans in 1461, leaving Elizabeth a widow. King Edward IV fell in love with her and married her in May 1464. Elizabeth died in June 1492 at Bermondsey Abbey.

Anne Neville: Daughter of Richard Neville, Earl of Warwick, in later centuries known as "the Kingmaker". Anne was the earl's second daughter and co-heiress. She was first married to Marguerite of Anjou's son, and shortly after his death, she married Richard, Duke of Gloucester. She died in March 1485 due to a mysterious illness that had been afflicting her for several months. Some contemporaries suggested she was poisoned.

Elizabeth of York: Daughter of Edward IV and Elizabeth Woodville. She married Henry VII in January 1486. Renowned for her beauty and charitable deeds, Elizabeth was a much beloved Queen, although some sources suggest that she was subjected to her mother-in-law's dominating will. Elizabeth bore eight children—the most famous of them all is Henry VIII. She died in February 1503 of childbed fever.

Selected members of the Beaufort family:

Margaret Beaufort: Henry VII's mother. She was married four times, though her first marriage was dissolved before it became lawfully binding.

Edmund Beaufort, 2nd Duke of Somerset: Margaret Beaufort's paternal uncle. Marguerite of Anjou aligned herself with him, and Edmund shared in her unpopularity. He was killed during the First Battle of St Albans in 1455.

Henry Beaufort, 3rd Duke of Somerset: An important Lancastrian commander and son of Edmund Beaufort. He was pardoned for his Lancastrian loyalties in 1462 and remained close to the Yorkist King, Edward IV. He would, eventually, return to the Lancastrian cause. He was executed after the Battle of Hexham in May 1464.

Edmund Beaufort, 4th Duke of Somerset: Brother of Henry Beaufort. After the defeat of the Lancastrian forces, which he commanded, he and the other leaders fled to the sanctuary within Tewkesbury Abbey. They were forced to leave the abbey and were immediately executed. Edmund's younger brother, John, who would have inherited the title of the Duke of Somerset, was killed during the battle. With the death of Edmund and John, the male Beaufort line became extinct.

Selected members of the Woodville family:

Jacquetta Woodville, Duchess of Bedford: Elizabeth Woodville's mother. Accused of witchcraft in 1469 during Warwick's rebellion, exonerated from charges in 1470.

Richard Woodville, Earl Rivers: Elizabeth Woodville's father. He was beheaded in August 1469 during Warwick's rebellion.

Anthony Woodville, 2nd Earl Rivers: One of Elizabeth Woodville's brothers and a governor of the Prince of Wales. He was beheaded in June 1483 on Richard III's orders.

Thomas Grey, Marquess of Dorset: Elizabeth Woodville's elder son from her first marriage.

Richard Grey: Elizabeth Woodville's younger son from her first marriage, executed in June 1483.

PART ONE:

Elizabeth Woodville

1. What did Elizabeth Woodville look like?

The sixteenth-century tradition has it that Elizabeth Woodville captured Edward IV's attention as she stood under an oak tree while the King was passing by. This young, impoverished widow, accompanied by her two small sons, was brave enough to personally petition the King to be granted the lands owed to her under the terms of her dowry. The King, who had found himself enamoured with Elizabeth's "beauty of person and charm of manner",[1] wanted to make her his mistress. Elizabeth, however, "virtuously denied him".[2] By all accounts, Elizabeth Woodville firmly stood her ground and was determined "to die rather than live unchastely with the King",[3] even when Edward placed a dagger at her throat to make her submit to his passion—or so the popular story goes. The young King

---

[1] Arlene Okerlund, *Elizabeth, England's Slandered Queen*, p. 17.
[2] Ibid., p. 16.
[3] Ibid., p. 17.

finally realized that he "could not corrupt her virtue by gifts or menaces",[4] so he decided to marry Elizabeth Woodville.

By marrying the King of England, Elizabeth Woodville became the first commoner Queen consort. Her royal title would put her in the midst of the Wars of the Roses; her father, two brothers and a son from her first marriage would be ruthlessly executed, and the fate of her two sons by Edward IV—the Princes in the Tower—would remain one of the most enduring historical mysteries. Perhaps even Elizabeth did not know what exactly happened to her sons. Her reputation, despite the fact that she refused to live unchastely as the King's mistress, was callously slandered during the course of history. Elizabeth Woodville was an unusual choice for a Queen of England; her nationality, social status and lack of virginity all challenged contemporary assumptions about medieval queenship, because kings did not usually marry for love. It seems, however, that Edward IV fell deeply in love with this widow who was five years his senior. This naturally raises the question of what Elizabeth Woodville looked like. In this chapter, we will take a close look at Elizabeth's appearance and the existing depictions of her.

---

[4] Ibid.

Conventions concerning feminine medieval beauty required women to have long blonde hair, fair skin, red lips, sparkling grey eyes and body features indicating fertility.[5] As for the rest of the body, to quote one medieval writer, Juan Ruiz, "Look for a woman with a good figure and with a small head; hair that is blonde but not from henna; whose eyebrows are spaced apart, long and arched in a peak; who is nice and plump in the buttocks: this is the figure of a lady".[6] Blonde hair reigned in the medieval hierarchy of beauty: the Virgin Mary, an ideal woman and a model of medieval queenship, was always portrayed as a blonde. Even medieval depictions of the biblical Queen of Sheba portrayed her with long blonde hair, although she was black-skinned.[7]

In the realm of historical fiction, Elizabeth Woodville is described as having "silver-gilt hair"[8]—in fact, the idea of silver-gilt hair has become so popular that it is often quoted as being a fact. Elizabeth Woodville's hair colour is nowhere recorded in historical sources, although contemporary

---

[5] Kim M. Philips, *Medieval Maidens: Young Women and Gender in England, c.1270-c.1540*, p. 45.
[6] Ronald Gabriel Benavides, *Chaucer, Ruiz and the Voices of Human Reason*, p. 384.
[7] L. Laynesmith, *The Last Medieval Queens*, p. 52.
[8] Rosemary Hawley Jarman, *The King's Grey Mare*, p. 1.
Josephine Tey, *The Daughter of Time*, p. 173.

illustrations—mostly in manuscripts—depict her with long blonde hair. One such contemporary image shows Elizabeth in similar robes to those in which the Virgin Mary was often portrayed. This picture is found in the records of the Skinners of London, produced in the 1470s to record Elizabeth's membership in their fraternity of the Assumption of the Virgin Mary. In this image, Elizabeth Woodville wears a red dress beneath a blue cloak—the red symbolizes her earthly nature and the blue her heavenly attributes—and loose blonde hair is falling down her back. Elizabeth is surrounded by gillyflowers and roses, flowers associated with the Virgin Mary; the rose standing for virginity, the gillyflower for purity and motherhood.[9] Because blonde hair was a particularly important physical attribute to fifteenth-century queens, it does not necessarily mean that Elizabeth Woodville was indeed blonde. Portraying a queen as a blonde may have been an attempt to present her as a perfect woman suitable to the role of a queen, even if her hair colour was different. The Milanese ambassador, for instance, described Elizabeth Woodville's predecessor, Marguerite of Anjou, as "a most handsome woman, though

---

[9] J. L. Laynesmith, The Last Medieval Queens, p. 33.

somewhat dark",[10] flattering his royal mistress, Bianca Maria Visconti, at the same time, assuring her that Marguerite was "not so beautiful as your Serenity". Although "somewhat dark" may imply that Marguerite's hair colour varied from dark blonde to dark brown, it may also refer to her skin tone. In any case, Marguerite of Anjou was always portrayed in contemporary illustrations as a blonde. Perhaps both Marguerite of Anjou and Elizabeth Woodville were depicted as blondes to fulfil the ideal and not to show their actual features. It is, however, possible that Elizabeth Woodville's hair was indeed blonde. Her eldest daughter, Elizabeth of York, had "fair yellow hair"[11] mentioned in the narrative of her coronation, and it is possible that she inherited the blonde locks from her mother.

The only portrait of Elizabeth Woodville that has survived to the present day is now located in the Queens' College, Cambridge, and it is believed to have been derived in the sixteenth century from a lost original. The existing portrait of Elizabeth Woodville was listed in the Royal Collection in 1542 and 1547—Henry VIII and Edward VI owned a portrait of Elizabeth, and it is highly possible that it

---

[10] *Calendar of State Papers and Manuscripts in the Archives and Collections of Milan*, note 1458.
[11] Sarah Gristwood, *Blood Sisters*, p. 264.

was the original painting.[12] In the portrait, which is featured on the cover of this book, Elizabeth wears a black gown with patterned collar and cuffs, a truncated hennin—a type of a medieval headdress with a butterfly veil—and a matching necklace.

Fifteenth-century fashion favoured displaying a high forehead, and some women plucked the hair on their foreheads and temples, and frequently also their eyebrows, to make their faces appear longer; Elizabeth clearly followed this fashion. As to Elizabeth's eyes, there is a famous quote circulating in some books stating that she had "heavy-lidded eyes like those of a dragon."[13] Unfortunately, this description belongs to the realm of fiction because it is not taken from a contemporary source.

Apart from contemporary illustrations and the portrait derived from a lost original, there are also representations of Elizabeth Woodville in stained glass. The eastern window in the Little Malvern Priory depicts the family of Edward IV, including Elizabeth Woodville and their children. The upper section of the Queen's figure, however, had been lost during the course of history. Stained glass in

---

[12] Jennifer Scott, *The Royal Portrait: Image and Impact*, p. 26.
[13] Jane Bingham, *The Cotswolds: A Cultural History*, p. 66.

the Canterbury Cathedral depicts Elizabeth Woodville, Edward IV and their children again—this particular representation of the Queen has been dated to 1482 and has survived to our times. There are also written descriptions of Elizabeth's appearance, and now we will take a closer look at them.

Dominic Mancini, who visited England in the summer of 1483, mentioned Elizabeth's "beauty of person and charm of manner" without getting into the details of her personal appearance. Another contemporary chronicler commented upon Elizabeth's "constant womanhood, wisdom and beauty",[14] although he, too, offered no details. Thomas More, a Tudor scholar and humanist who was writing some twenty years after Elizabeth Woodville's death, stated that she was "both fair and of a good favour, moderate of stature, well made and very wise".[15] Edward Hall, who started writing his chronicle in 1535, stated that Elizabeth "was a woman more of formal countenance, than of excellent beauty, but yet of such fresh beauty and favour, that with her sober demeanour, lovely looking, and feminine

---

[14] Arlene Okerlund, *Elizabeth, England's Slandered Queen*, p. 17.
[15] Ibid., p. 15.

smiling (neither too wanton nor too humble) . . . she allured and made subject to her the heart of so great a King".[16]

Enamoured with Elizabeth Woodville's beauty and eloquence, the young Edward IV decided to defy tradition and marry one of his subjects. Elizabeth's beauty was commonly assumed to be a major factor in Edward IV's decision, since Elizabeth was a widow with two small sons and the daughter of a man who was previously berated by Edward for his low birth. Edward IV's contemporaries were so shocked at the news of his marriage to Elizabeth Woodville that they assumed witchcraft was involved! It was hard to understand why the young King, who was supposed to forge an international alliance and strengthen his own newly achieved, fragile position, decided to marry a woman five years his senior, a mere commoner, and on top of that, a widow with Lancastrian ties!

Being an Englishwoman of no royal blood, Elizabeth Woodville could not offer a large dowry or secure a strong international alliance, though both would have been very useful to a King who had won the crown by conquest. By rejecting the possibility of a foreign bride, Edward IV offended many nobles of his realm, and by promoting the

---

[16] Sarah Gristwood, *Blood Sisters*, p. 84.

large family of his beautiful wife, he was partly responsible for later rebellions and feuds. Despite all the obstacles, however, Edward IV married Elizabeth Woodville on 1 May 1464 and presented her as his wife several months later. Their union lasted for nineteen years and produced ten children. But Elizabeth's huge family was never popular in England during Edward IV's reign, mainly because the King married the Woodvilles into the nobility and relied on their advice more than he relied on the advice of his former allies. The Woodville family's infamous reputation is further discussed in the next chapter.

2. The Woodvilles, a family raised high

Edward IV's choice of bride stunned the nation because the young King challenged the structure of society; instead of marrying a foreign bride who could bring new alliances, he married an Englishwoman of relatively low birth. Considering the fact that Edward IV was a King who had achieved the crown by conquest—at the time of his highly unpopular marriage, he was in the third year of his reign—his choice of bride was both shocking and politically dangerous. Elizabeth Woodville did not fulfil contemporary expectations of potential queens because she was an Englishwoman of low birth, she was not a virgin and the King married her for love rather than for political benefits. All those factors challenged contemporary assumptions about queenship and made Elizabeth Woodville and her family very unpopular figures.

The Burgundian chronicler, Jean de Waurin, reported the mood in England when Edward IV presented Elizabeth Woodville as his wife: "They [nobility of the realm] answered that she was not his match, that however good and fair she might be, she was not a wife for so high a prince as he; and he knew this well, for she was not the daughter of a duke or earl, but her mother had married a simple knight, so that though she was the daughter of the Duchess of Bedford and the niece of the Count of Saint-Pol, she was no wife for him."[1] The clandestine nature of his courtship and marriage indicates that Edward IV knew very well that Elizabeth Woodville was not great material for a queen due to her humble origin.

Only four years earlier, in January 1460, young Edward had an interesting encounter with his future wife's family, when Sir Richard Woodville, Elizabeth's father, and his eldest son, Anthony, were organising Lancastrian troops at Sandwich to attack Calais—controlled at the time by the Earl of Warwick's Yorkist troops. They were captured and handed over to the three leaders of the Yorkist faction: the Earl of Warwick (today known as "the Kingmaker"), Lord Salisbury, and the future King Edward IV, back then holding the title of the Earl of March. The three Yorkists taunted the Woodvilles: Lord Salisbury berated Richard Woodville, "calling him a knave's son", and the Earl of Warwick added that "his father was but a squire and brought up with King

---

[1] Arlene Okerlund, *Elizabeth, Englands Slandered Queen*, p. 60.

Henry V". Richard Woodville's greatest offence, in the Earl of Warwick's opinion, was the fact that Woodville had married outside of his social status: his wife was Jacquetta of Luxembourg, widow of John, Duke of Bedford and sister-in-law to the Lancastrian King Henry VI. According to Warwick, Richard Woodville was a man without nobility of blood who became Lord Rivers through the agency of his influential wife and was promoted far beyond his proper place. The future King Edward, "rated him in likewise".[2] It was an irony in itself that Edward IV later married the daughter of the man he had ridiculed for his low birth!

Was Elizabeth Woodville's origin indeed low? Back in the medieval times, it was parentage that defined nobility. Although Elizabeth's mother, Jacquetta, was the daughter of Pierre of Luxembourg, Count of Saint-Pol, and a widow of the Duke of Bedford, she could not share her rank with her children.[3] A woman's status came from her father, and Elizabeth Woodville's father was merely a knight, recently elevated to the title of Lord Rivers.[4]

---

[2] Alice Drayton Greenwood, Selections From the Paston Letters as Transcribed by Sir John Fenn, p. 141.
[3] Sarah Gristwood, *Blood Sisters*, p. 88.
[4] J. L. Laynesmith, *The Last Medieval Queens*, p. 53.

Seventeen-year-old Jacquetta married the Duke of Bedford, brother to Henry V and uncle to Henry VI, in April 1433, and thus she became one of the most important women at the English court. The young Jacquetta met her future husband, Richard Woodville, while he served in the Duke of Bedford's household—we can only imagine how the secret love grew between the young couple.

Before the Duke of Bedford died on 15 September 1435, he made sure that his young widow was well provided for; Jacquetta was granted her dower on 6 February 1436 under condition she would not remarry without royal permission. Jacquetta, however, broke this condition and married Richard Woodville. As the daughter of the Count of Saint-Pol and the widow of a duke, Jacquetta was a great catch, and Richard Woodville, being a simple knight, was not her social equal. It seems that this marriage was a love match and the young Jacquetta was determined to shape her own destiny—perhaps she was emboldened to marry for love when she saw the Queen Dowager, Catherine of Valois, married to her squire, Owen Tudor. If a former Queen could marry for love, why couldn't Jacquetta?

Such a marriage, however, did not come cheaply since Jacquetta married without a licence and had to suffer the consequences. Jacquetta and Richard Woodville admitted that they suffered both "in their persons as in their goods" and petitioned King Henry VI to set a reasonable fine.[5] The fine was set at £1,000, a considerable sum in the fifteenth century.[6] The couple was eventually pardoned and welcomed at court.

Both Jacquetta and her new husband found favour with Henry VI, who sent them together with the royal entourage to bring his bride, Marguerite of Anjou, from France. The Woodvilles established themselves as loyal Lancastrians; Jacquetta became Marguerite's principal lady-in-waiting and friend, while her husband was given the title of Baron Rivers and fought on the side of the House of Lancaster.

Edward IV's choice of bride shocked not only the nobility of England but also the foreign monarchs and ambassadors. Among Edward's potential foreign brides was Isabella of Castile, who—decades later—still harboured resentment towards Edward IV for choosing "a widow of England"[7] instead of her. In 1469, the Milanese ambassador

---

[5] Arlene Okerlund, *Elizabeth, England's Slandered Queen*, p. 40.
[6] David Baldwin, *Elizabeth Woodville: Mother of the Princes in the Tower*, p. 2.
[7] Arlene Okerlund, *Elizabeth, England's Slandered Queen*, p. 32.

reported that "the King here took to wife a widow of this island of quite low birth."[8] Dominic Mancini described the animosity towards the marriage as a product of "antagonism of the magnates of the kingdom, who disdained to show royal honours towards an undistinguished woman promoted to such exalted rank".[9]

While Edward IV's marriage is usually ascribed to his infatuation with Elizabeth Woodville, some historians have suggested that this marriage was politically motivated. B. Wilkinson in *Constitutional History of England* argued that Edward wanted to free himself from under the Earl of Warwick's influence and made an attempt to build a new court party and assert his independence from his powerful cousin.[10] It could also be argued that Edward IV wanted to avoid marrying a French bride, knowing that the previous French Queen consort, Marguerite of Anjou, was perceived as a "vengeful and violent woman"[11] who was a "threat to Englishness."[12] It is equally possible that by marrying a woman with long-standing Lancastrian ties—not only were

---

[8] *Calendar of State Papers and Manuscripts in the Archives and Collections of Milan*, note 173.

[9] Mancini, *The Usurpation of Richard III,* p. 61.

[10] Charles Ross, *Edward IV*, p. 87.

[11] H. E. Maurer, *Margaret of Anjou: Queenship and Power in Late Medieval England*, p. 1.

[12] J. L. Laynesmith, *The Last Medieval Queens*, p. 46.

Elizabeth's parents former Lancastrians but her first husband also fought for the Lancastrian cause and died at the Second Battle of St Albans in 1461—Edward IV was eager to secure the support of other ex-Lancastrians.[13]

Whatever the motivation behind Edward IV's marriage to Elizabeth Woodville, she and her family became notoriously disliked and were perceived as greedy parvenus. The Milanese ambassador reported that Elizabeth "had always exerted herself to aggrandize her relations . . . they had the entire government of the realm."[14] The Woodvilles were a large, close-knit clan: Elizabeth was the oldest of fifteen children born to Richard and Jacquetta, thirteen of whom survived to adulthood.[15] The aggrandizement of the Woodville family mentioned by the Milanese ambassador started in the mid-1460s and was achieved mostly through marriages of Elizabeth's brothers, sisters and cousins into the high ranks of the English nobility. The Woodvilles were soon linked to powerful noble families and they were accused of obtaining the best possible marriages.

One of Elizabeth's sisters, Katherine, married the Duke of Buckingham and, as a contemporary observer

---

[13] J. L. Laynesmith, *The Last Medieval Queens*, p. 57.

[14] Sarah Gristwood, *Blood Sisters*, p. 99.

[15] Arlene Okerlund, *Elizabeth of York*, p. 46.

reported, the Duke "had been forced to marry the Queen's sister, whom he scorned to wed on account of her humble origin".[16] Elizabeth Woodville's eldest son, Thomas Grey, Marquess of Dorset, married Edward IV's niece, Anne Holland, whose hand in marriage had previously been promised to the Earl of Warwick's cousin, George Neville.

One of the most scandalous Woodville marriages was the union between Elizabeth's youngest brother, John, who at the age of twenty married the elderly Duchess of Norfolk, Edward IV's aunt, who had already survived three husbands and would, ironically, survive her young spouse, who was executed in 1469.[17] One of the contemporary chroniclers scornfully referred to the duchess as "a slip of a girl about eighty years old",[18] although she was about sixty at that time. Such an exaggeration served to point out the Woodville family's ruthlessness in achieving their goals; the marriage was deemed as "diabolical",[19] although there is no evidence that the elderly duchess was in any way forced to become John Woodville's wife.

---

[16] Mancini, *The Usurpation of Richard III*, p. 75.

[17] Arlene Okerlund, *Elizabeth, England's Slandered Queen*, p. 78.

[18] Keith Dockray, *Edward IV: A Sourcebook*, p. 48.

[19] Ibid.

As to Elizabeth Woodville's sisters, they married men who were expected to inherit earldoms: Anne married William, Viscount Bourchier, eldest son and heir of the Earl of Essex, and Eleanor became the wife of Anthony Grey, heir of the Earl of Kent.[20]

These marriages caused damage to Elizabeth Woodville's reputation because she was seen as a driving force behind them. In her book, *Elizabeth: England's Slandered Queen*, Arlene Okerlund makes a valid point when she points out that "The fact that the Queen was blamed for the marriages, when they clearly required the King's participation and approval, remains a curiosity of perspective".[21] The example of earlier kings as well as the convention of the times obliged Edward IV to take care of his wife's relatives,[22] yet it was Elizabeth Woodville who was blamed the most for her family's elevation.

This perception is not entirely baseless, however, because in October of 1466, for example, the Queen paid 4,000 marks to Edward IV's sister, the Duchess of Exeter, for the marriage of her eldest son, Thomas Grey, to Anne

---

[20] Charles Ross, *Edward IV*, p. 93.
[21] Arlene Okerlund, *Elizabeth, England's Slandered Queen*, p. 76.
[22] David Baldwin, *Elizabeth Woodville*, p. 21.

Holland, the duchess's only daughter.[23] Elizabeth Woodville could, perhaps, be held responsible for suggesting the marriages, but as one of the contemporaries pointed out, it was the King who was ultimately in charge: "The King caused Henry, Duke of Buckingham, to marry a sister of Queen Elizabeth [Katherine] to the secret displeasure of the Earl of Warwick".[24]

Elizabeth naturally promoted the interests of her family (who can blame her?), raising its members to familiarity with the King. She was seen as the representative of the Woodville clan and became a highly unpopular figure. The nobles of the realm were outraged at the rapid ennoblement of the Woodvilles as much as they were displeased with Edward IV's decision to marry a widow of low birth in utmost secrecy. All those factors coupled together, created a dangerous mixture of festering resentment that would eventually lead to open rebellion against Edward IV.

Richard Neville, Earl of Warwick, "the Kingmaker", was England's greatest magnate. He was also Edward IV's cousin and the man who helped the nineteen-year-old King

---

[23] Arlene Okerlund, *Elizabeth, England's Slandered Queen*, p. 77.
[24] Keith Dockray, *Edward IV: a Sourcebook*, p. 48.

win the crown. After his return from France, where he had been negotiating the terms of a marriage between Edward IV and Bona of Savoy, he found out that Edward had married Elizabeth Woodville. Although Warwick harboured resentment towards Edward IV, he was able to move on and accept the new Queen. He found himself, however, unable to accept the new Queen's "overweening influence with the King"[25] and the sudden elevation of the Woodville family through many marriages. As historian Charles Ross pointed out, Warwick "could justly feel aggrieved about the implications of these marriages for the prospects of his own heirs, his two daughters, Isabel and Anne Neville".[26] The Kingmaker's daughters were the richest heiresses in England, but there were no suitable candidates for their husbands since the most eligible bachelors had already been claimed by Elizabeth Woodville's female relatives. Additionally, Edward IV refused to grant permission for Warwick's daughters to marry his brothers, George and Richard. Elizabeth Woodville and her family thus became a target of Warwick's anger.

Matters came to head in 1469 when the powerful Earl rebelled and allied himself with Edward IV's younger

---

[25] Charles Ross, *Richard III*, p. 12.
[26] Charles Ross, *Edward IV*, p. 94.

brother, George, the Duke of Clarence. Their anger was aimed directly against "the deceitful, covetous rule and guiding of certain seditious persons"[27]—the Woodville family and their adherents. In July 1469, Warwick married his elder daughter, Isabel, to the Duke of Clarence, and defeated Edward IV, imprisoning him in his estate.

In August of that year, Warwick and Clarence were spreading the rumour that Edward IV was a product of his mother's adulterous affair, and thus he was not the rightful heir to the throne. Warwick's motive was plain: he planned to dethrone Edward IV and replace him with his brother, George, who had conveniently married Warwick's daughter. The rebellion had dramatic consequences for Elizabeth Woodville's family: her father, Sir Richard Woodville, and younger brother, John, were beheaded without trial on Warwick's orders in August 1469. The Queen's mother was accused of witchcraft, and Elizabeth Woodville's own position was endangered.

The Earl of Warwick, however, was not as lucky as he expected to be, and due to lack of support, he released Edward IV from captivity in September 1469. The King returned to his court, and a special commission exonerated

---

[27] Elizabeth Norton, *Margaret Beaufort*, p. 84.

his mother-in-law from the charges of witchcraft. Despite everything Warwick and Clarence had done, Edward IV pardoned and welcomed the former traitors at court. The truce was short-lived, however, and in April 1470, Warwick and Clarence allied themselves with the Lancastrian queen-in-exile, Marguerite of Anjou. The plan was to restore Henry VI to the throne. In order to seal the deal, Warwick's younger daughter, Anne Neville, married Marguerite of Anjou's son, Prince Edward. Warwick invaded England and freed Henry VI from the Tower of London, while Edward IV was forced to leave his country and go into exile. Elizabeth Woodville, eight months pregnant at that time, gathered her children and entered the Westminster Sanctuary.

Edward IV eventually returned to reclaim his throne in March 1471. George, Duke of Clarence, realizing that he should join his brother, who was enthusiastically welcomed in England, begged his forgiveness and was pardoned. The people of England did not want to see the frail and mentally unstable King Henry VI on the throne—young, energetic Edward IV seemed a far better option.

Edward marched towards London and encountered no resistance. The languid King Henry VI was send to the Tower yet again, and on 12 April 1471, Edward IV was reunited with his wife in the sanctuary. Not only did he see the faces of his beloved Queen and their daughters—he saw, for the first time, his son, who had been born in sanctuary five months earlier. The birth of the first male heir to the Yorkist throne seemed like a miracle and a sign that God looked favourably upon Edward IV's reign. Two days later, at the Battle of Barnet, the Earl of Warwick was killed, his death putting an end to his ambitions. But the battle was not yet over, since Marguerite of Anjou still harboured hope that her son would reclaim his inheritance. Unfortunately for Marguerite, her army was crushed at Tewkesbury on 4 May 1471, and her only son was killed.

The brave queen was imprisoned in the Tower, and on 21 May, her husband, the hapless Henry VI, died in unclear circumstances. Although *The Arrival of Edward IV*, more Yorkist in sympathy, says that Henry VI died "of pure displeasure and melancholy"[28] upon hearing the news about the defeat of his armies and his son's death, there are several contemporary sources which claim that the Lancastrian king was murdered. With his rivals either dead or imprisoned, the victorious King Edward IV began twelve years of uninterrupted rule.

---

[28] David Baldwin, *Richard III*, p. 56.

During those years, Queen Elizabeth Woodville bore more children and her family continued to bask in the sunshine of royal favour. Their good fortunes ended suddenly with Edward IV's death on 9 April 1483. The King was merely forty years old, and his death came as a huge shock both to his family and subjects. Some sources claimed that Edward died due to overindulgence in food and drink; some even suggested poisoning. Contemporary observer, Dominic Mancini, reported that the King went fishing and caught a cold.[29] Whatever the cause, Edward IV died and left his twelve-year-old son as heir. Here, again, the unpopularity of the Woodvilles had serious ramifications for Elizabeth herself, her children and other members of her clan.

Shortly after Edward IV's death, his son, Edward V, set out from Ludlow Castle to London. He was surrounded by his Woodville relatives and their adherents. Among them was Anthony Woodville, the Queen's brother, who carried his executed father's title, Earl Rivers, and Sir Richard Grey, Elizabeth Woodville's son from her first marriage. Anthony Woodville was Edward V's governor—a supervisor and mentor who took care of the boy's education—and renowned for his piety, scholarly achievements, military

---

[29] Sarah Gristwood, *Blood Sisters*, p. 173.

skills and political acumen. Dominic Mancini reported that Anthony was "always considered a kind, serious, and just man, and one tested by every vicissitude of life. Whatever his prosperity, he had injured nobody, though benefitting many; and therefore he [Edward IV] had entrusted to him the care and direction of the King's eldest son".[30]

While Edward V was heading to London, the Duke of Gloucester also set out from his northern estates, surrounded by his servants and one of his new allies, Henry Stafford, the Duke of Buckingham. According to Dominic Mancini, the two parties—one headed by Anthony Woodville and the other headed by Gloucester—decided to meet along the way. Anthony Woodville and Richard Grey rode out to meet with the Dukes of Gloucester and Buckingham in Northampton, leaving Edward V behind in Stony Stratford. The men spent a congenial evening "in very pleasant conversation".[31]

The next morning, however, Anthony Woodville and Richard Grey were suddenly arrested, while the Dukes of Gloucester and Buckingham "hastened at full gallop towards

---

[30] Dominic Mancini, *The Usurpation of Richard III*, p. 69.
[31] The Crowland Chronicle
http://newr3.dreamhosters.com/?page_id=518

the young King".[32] As the dukes arrived, they arrested more servants who attended Edward V, including Thomas Vaughan, his chamberlain. Both Gloucester and Buckingham exhibited a "mournful countenance, while expressing profound grief at the death of the King's father" and accused Edward IV's ministers of having "little regard for his honour, since they were accounted the companions and servants of his vices, and had ruined his health".[33]

Here, the dukes were referring to Edward IV's immoral lifestyle, for he was famous for his licentiousness.[34] It was common knowledge at court that Edward IV's companions in his wanton behaviour were "three of the aforementioned relatives of the Queen, her two sons and one of her brothers"[35]—Thomas and Richard Grey and Edward Woodville. The dukes, afraid that the same would happen to Edward V, requested that "these ministers should be removed from the King's side". The Duke of Gloucester also accused the said ministers of "conspiring his death and preparing ambushes both in the capital and on the road".

---

[32] Dominic Mancini, *The Usurpation of Richard III*, p. 77.
[33] Ibid.
[34] Ibid., p. 67.
[35] Ibid.

Moreover, he said that they attempted to deprive him of the office of regent, which Edward IV had conferred on him, and that he believed himself able to "discharge all the duties of government"[36] because he was more experienced and popular. The young King replied that he trusted in those men whom his father had given him and that he "had seen nothing evil in them and wished to keep them."[37] Then, Edward V invoked his mother's name, saying that "he had complete confidence in the peers of the realm and the Queen". The Duke of Buckingham, who loathed the Queen's family, angrily replied that "it was not the business of women to govern kingdoms"[38] and Edward V should relinquish any hope he had in his mother. The young monarch, seeing that his resistance was pointless, had no other choice but to obey the dukes' demands.

When the Queen learned that her son was in the Duke of Gloucester's custody and members of her family were imprisoned, she—together with her second son from her first marriage, Thomas Grey, Marquess of Dorset—tried to raise an army but encountered opposition. Dominic Mancini, who witnessed the events of the spring of 1483 as

---

[36] Ibid., p. 77.
[37] Ibid.
[38] Ibid.

they unfolded, reported that "when they [the Queen and the Marquess of Dorset] had exhorted certain nobles who had come to the City, and others, to take up arms, they perceived that men's minds were not only irresolute but altogether hostile to themselves."[39]

Without the protection of her royal husband, Elizabeth Woodville was helpless. She must have been shocked when she learned that "some even said openly that it was more just and profitable that the youthful sovereign should be with his paternal uncle [Richard, Duke of Gloucester] than with his maternal uncles and uterine brothers".[40] With her own position fragile, she could not protect the interests of her family. Elizabeth did what had worked once before: she gathered all of her daughters, Prince Richard, Duke of York, and, accompanied by the Marquess of Dorset, hurried into the Westminster Sanctuary.

The coronation of Edward V, scheduled for 4 May 1483, never took place. That day, the royal entourage reached London accompanied by the Dukes of Gloucester and Buckingham. They received a heartfelt welcome from

---

[39] Ibid., p. 79.
[40] Ibid.

the Lord Mayor, aldermen and about five hundred citizens, and, as Mancini claimed, "these two dukes were seeking at every turn to arouse hatred against the Queen's kin, and to estrange the public opinion from her relatives".[41]

The Duke of Gloucester then sent letters to the council, claiming that Elizabeth Woodville and her family "have intended and daily doth intend to murder and utterly destroy us and our cousin the Duke of Buckingham and the old royal blood of this realm".[42] Four cartloads of weapons were put in front of Edward V's procession during his entry to London—Gloucester claimed that they had been stored by the Woodvilles, who intended to use them against him. Mancini wrote that "many knew these charges to be false"[43] since the weapons had been stored when war was being waged against Scotland.

Having custody of Edward V, Richard of Gloucester started working his own way to the throne. On 13 June 1483, Lord Hastings, Edward IV's close friend and chamberlain, was executed without trial. Then, Gloucester convinced Elizabeth Woodville to release her younger son, the Duke of York, and she—persuaded by the Archbishop of

---

[41] Ibid., p. 83.

[42] Arlene Okerlund, *Elizabeth: England's Slandered Queen*, p. 213.

[43] Dominic Mancini, *The Usurpation of Richard III*, p. 83.

Canterbury, who promised that no harm would befall her sons—agreed. Three days later, the Duke of York joined his elder brother in the Tower of London. They were seen playing outside the Tower's walls, enjoying the beautiful sunny weather, but in the summer of 1483, the princes ceased to appear altogether, and the common belief is that they were murdered around that time.

The Duke of Gloucester quickly made his intentions clear and soon informed the nation that his brother's marriage to Elizabeth Woodville was invalid because of Edward IV's pre-contract to Lady Eleanor Butler. The pre-contract issue is still hotly debated among scholars today; whether it really existed or not is irrelevant since the Duke of Gloucester reached his goal and assumed the crown on that account.

In January 1484, Richard III's only parliament enacted the bill known as *Titulus Regius*, which justified his claim to the throne. The bill proclaimed Elizabeth Woodville's marriage to Edward IV as an adulterous and unlawful union due to Edward's pre-contract. The children born out of this "sinful and damnable adultery" were thus "unable to inherit or to claim anything by inheritance".[44]

---

[44] Sarah Gristwood, *Blood Sisters*, p. 213.

Furthermore, Elizabeth Woodville was accused of witchcraft and sorcery, and her deceased mother—Jacquetta died in 1472—was named as her accomplice.

Some sources state that Richard of Gloucester's claim to the throne was also based on the assumption that Edward IV himself was a bastard borne out of Cecily Neville's adulterous affair. Such rumours circulated in 1469, and according to Mancini, Cecily herself, upon hearing about Edward's marriage to a low-born widow, declared that Edward was not the son of her husband. *Titulus Regius*, however, did not mention the issue of Edward IV's alleged bastardy, and considering the fact that this document justified Richard's claim to the throne, it would have certainly done so if that were the case.

On 25 June 1483, Anthony Woodville, the Queen's brother, Richard Grey, her son from first marriage, and Thomas Vaughan, Edward V's chamberlain, were executed at Pontefract Castle. Anthony Woodville was known as an erudite and pious man, and he had been a constant presence in Edward V's life since 1473. A little less is known about Elizabeth Woodville's younger son from her first marriage. Dominic Mancini described Richard Grey as "quite young"[45] while *The Crowland Chronicle* said he was "a most noble knight".[46] He never married and left no children—or at least none that we know of. Thomas Vaughan was the eldest man executed that day. In his mid-fifties, he had loyally served at court for years. Vaughan had become a member of the Edward V's council in Ludlow Castle and served in the capacity of the chamberlain.

According to *The Crowland Chronicle*, the victims were not accorded a formal trial, although John Rous, also a contemporary observer, recorded that the Earl of Northumberland was their "chief judge".[47] Two days before those executions took place, Anthony Woodville made his will and wrote a ballad in which he demonstrated that he was willing to die—he probably assumed that he would die anyway since the Duke of Gloucester had made his intentions clear.

All contemporary observers agreed that the executions were unjust. Rous remarked that the victims were "lamented by almost all and innocent of the deed

---

[45] Dominic Mancini, *The Usurpation of Richard III*, p. 79.
[46] The Crowland Chronicle
http://newr3.dreamhosters.com/?page_id=518
[47] Keith Dockray, *Richard III: A Source Book*, p. 52.

charged against them"[48] while *The Crowland Chronicle* concluded that "this was the second innocent blood which was shed on the occasion of this sudden change."[49]

Upon eliminating his enemies and neutralising potential heirs to the throne, the Duke of Gloucester was crowned as Richard III on 6 July 1483. It would be no exaggeration to say that the unpopularity of Elizabeth Woodville and her kin contributed to Richard III's usurpation. The young Edward V had grown up surrounded by his maternal relatives and Woodville beneficiaries, and the power during the young king's minority would have been held by the unpopular Woodvilles.

Most of the nobility of the realm did not welcome this prospect, and many were prepared to unite despite the hatred they bore each other to destroy the Woodvilles and limit their power after Edward IV's death. Furthermore, the painful memories of war were still fresh in everyone's minds, and no one wanted history to repeat itself. The nobility wanted to see an adult man reputed for his military abilities holding power rather than a young boy controlled by his maternal family, who were perceived as parvenus.

---

[48] Ibid.
[49] The Crowland Chronicle
http://newr3.dreamhosters.com/?page_id=518

This does not necessarily mean that Richard III's usurpation was welcomed: he was supposed to assume custody of Edward V and not wrest the throne from him.

Conclusion

Elizabeth Woodville was an unusual choice for a bride in every possible aspect. Her nationality, social status and lack of virginity challenged the ideology of medieval queenship.[50] Her family was perceived as acquisitive upstarts due to a series of marriages to members of higher nobility, their rapid social elevation and positions in close proximity to the King. The Queen was blamed for arranging the marriages for her siblings and cousins, and the unpopularity of the Woodville clan contributed to the political tension and division between the English nobility.

Had Edward IV married a foreign bride who could have secured a diplomatic alliance, perhaps the Wars of the Roses would have come to an end. However, he chose Elizabeth Woodville and contributed to the promotion of her family. It had serious ramifications for Edward IV himself (he became less popular than he had been before his

---

[50] J. L. Laynesmith, *The Last Medieval Queens*, p. 40.

marriage), his wife and her family. The Queen's unpopularity enabled the brief restoration of the Lancastrian King Henry VI in 1471 and helped bring about Richard III's usurpation in 1483.

Elizabeth Woodville paid dearly for her queenly rank: her father, brothers and sons were executed or vanished under mysterious circumstances. She sought refuge within the walls of sanctuary twice, faced witchcraft charges and survived many tribulations. And all of this because the King of England fell in love with her and deemed her worthy to become his wife and Queen. Was it love or was it sorcery? Their contemporaries often asked themselves this question, and some even directly accused Elizabeth Woodville of dabbling in witchcraft. Did Queen Elizabeth Woodville really engage in witchcraft? You will find the answer in the next chapter.

3. Elizabeth, witchcraft charges and the legendary Melusine

In January 1484, Richard III's only parliament enacted the bill known as *Titulus Regius* which justified his claim to the throne. According to this bill, Elizabeth Woodville and her mother had procured Elizabeth's marriage to Edward IV by witchcraft. It was not, however, the first time accusations of witchcraft had come up in connection with the Woodville women. In this chapter, we will take a closer look at those charges and try to establish how plausible they were and what evidence was offered to prove that Elizabeth and her mother dabbled in the dark arts.

The secret wedding

The circumstances of the first meeting between Elizabeth Woodville and Edward IV are unclear. According to chronicler Edward Hall, Edward IV visited the manor of Grafton, the Woodville family seat, while on a hunt in the forest of Wychwood. Thomas More, who recounted the meeting, claimed that Elizabeth "made a humble suit unto the King that she might be restored unto such small lands as her late husband had given her in jointure",[1] and the King fell in love with her.

The Victorian historian Agnes Strickland placed the meeting under an oak tree, where Elizabeth Woodville "addressed the young monarch, holding her fatherless boys by the hands, and when Edward paused to listen to her, she threw herself at his feet and pleaded earnestly for the restoration of Bradgate, the inheritance of her children".[2] Strickland adds that the tree, known as "the Queen's Oak", "was the scene of more than one interview between the beautiful Elizabeth and the enamoured Edward" and gave the direct location: "between Grafton and the Whittlebury

---

[1] Arlene Okerlund, *Elizabeth, England's Slandered Queen*, p. 15.
[2] Ibid., p. 24.

Forest".[3] Today, the legend still lives on and "the Queen's Oak", although it is probably not the same tree that stood tall in the 1460s, is found between Potterspury and Grafton Regis.[4]

As to the question of when exactly Elizabeth Woodville and Edward IV first met, there are various theories. There is evidence that Edward IV visited the Woodville family seat in Grafton as early as June 1461, and shortly before he left he issued a pardon for Elizabeth's father for his Lancastrian loyalties (Richard Woodville's goods were confiscated soon after the Battle of Towton).[5] Anthony Woodville, Elizabeth's brother, was also pardoned the following month, in July 1461, and from that moment on the Woodvilles were loyal to the new Yorkist king. Cora Scofield has argued that these pardons were made at Elizabeth Woodville's request, and, as J. L. Laynesmith pointed out, there is strong evidence to support this theory: the Burgundian chronicler Jean de Waurin attributed Richard Woodville's pardon to Edward IV's love for Elizabeth, his daughter.[6]

---

[3] Ibid.

[4] Ibid., p. 25.

[5] David Baldwin, *Elizabeth Woodville*, p. 8.

[6] J. L. Laynesmith, *The Last Medieval Queens*, p. 65.

Starting with Polydore Vergil, who claimed that Edward IV was "led by blind affection, and not by rule of reason"[7] when he married Elizabeth Woodville, subsequent historians have generally agreed that Edward's relationship with Elizabeth was "the impulsive love match of an impetuous young man".[8] Not all contemporary sources, however, confirm that the marriage was a product of a "blind affection" or that it was "impulsive". In October 1464, the Milanese ambassador reported that "the King of England has taken to wife an English lady, they say out of love".[9]

Another letter from October 1464 suggests that Edward IV was "determined to take the daughter of my Lord de Rivers, a widow with two children, having long loved her, it appears."[10] The contemporary chronicle stated that the King fell in love with Elizabeth when he "dined with her frequently" and Thomas More, although not a contemporary, confirmed this when he wrote that "many a meeting, much wooing, and many great promises" were

---

[7] Charles Ross, *Edward IV*, p. 92.
[8] Ibid., p. 86.
[9] J. L. Laynesmith, *The Last Medieval Queens*, p. 62.
[10] Ibid., p. 39.

involved in the courtship.[11] The legend about the romantic meeting under an oak tree is most probably that—a legend. It is more probable that Edward IV—who met Elizabeth as early as 1461—fell in love with her gradually, as she visited the court on occasion.

It is traditionally believed that Edward IV married Elizabeth Woodville on 1 May 1464. The clandestine nature of this ceremony led Richard III's parliament to claim that the wedding was procured "by sorcery and witchcraft, committed by the said Elizabeth and her mother, Jacquetta, Duchess of Bedford."[12] According to the act, witchcraft by Elizabeth and Jacquetta was "the common opinion of the people and the public voice, and the fame is through all this land".[13]

Considering the fact that Richard III wrested the throne from Elizabeth Woodville's son and proclaimed her marriage to Edward IV invalid due to the King's previous pre-contract with another woman, it is hardly surprising that Richard had decided to slander Elizabeth's name and accuse her of witchcraft. We should not forget that back in

---

[11] Arlene Okerlund, *Elizabeth Woodville, England's Slandered Queen*, p. 29.
[12] Titulus Regius http://www.richard111.com/titulus_regius.htm
[13] Ibid.

medieval times, witchcraft was a serious charge, and people tended to believe in the existence of witches and feared their influence. As historian Amy Licence pointed out, women were "more likely to be attacked on moral, superstitious and cultural grounds" and that "it was an emotive and easy charge to level against an enemy who was immune from, or innocent of, other potential slurs".[14]

The accusations of witchcraft surrounded Edward IV's marriage to Elizabeth Woodville and placed the responsibility squarely at the feet of Jacquetta Woodville's sorcery. "What obloquy ran after of his marriage, how the King was enchanted by the duchess of Bedford, I here pass over",[15] wrote Robert Fabyan in his chronicle. It is easy to see why Jacquetta was accused of "enchanting" Edward IV into marrying her daughter: Elizabeth was a shocking choice for a royal bride, and the circumstances of the wedding imply that Jacquetta played a prominent role in the ceremony and in what happened afterwards.

According to Fabyan's chronicle, none were present during the clandestine wedding, but "the spouses, the Duchess of Bedford, her [Elizabeth's] mother, the priest, two

---

[14] Amy Licence, *Elizabeth of York*, p. 51.
[15] Robert Fabyan, *The new chronicles of England and France*, p. 654.

gentlewomen, and a young man to help the priest sing." After the ceremony, Elizabeth "nightly to his [Edward's] bed was brought, in so secret manner that almost none but her mother was of counsel".[16] Because the wedding took place in a "most secret manner", as Fabyan recounted, Richard III's *Titulus Regius* may not have been that far from the truth when it asserted that the ceremony was held "in a private chamber, a profane place, and not openly in the face of the church."[17]

Although Richard III stated that the charge of witchcraft against Elizabeth Woodville "shall be proved sufficiently in time and place convenient",[18] he never offered any proof to confirm Elizabeth's and Jacquetta's guilt. It is possible that, as historian David Baldwin pointed out, Richard III intended to bring forward the old accusations levelled against Jacquetta Woodville, although the Queen's mother had been exonerated from witchcraft charges in 1470.[19]

The fact that the wedding ceremony took place in May, a month commonly associated with love, possibly

---

[16] Ibid.

[17] Titulus Regius http://www.richard111.com/titulus_regius.htm

[18] Ibid.

[19] David Baldwin, *Elizabeth Woodville*, p. 154.
  Calendar of Patent Rolls, 1467-77, p. 190.

originating from pre-Christian traditional celebrations of fertility[20], led to a series of surprising theories. According to W.E. Hampton, the wedding followed Edward IV's attendance at St Walpurga's Eve festival, while Annette Carson suggested that Edward IV could have been fed with a love potion.[21] The more plausible explanation though, is that Edward IV simply fell in love with Elizabeth Woodville.

Other accusations

In 1469, when the powerful Earl of Warwick rebelled against Edward IV, Jacquetta Woodville was officially charged with practising sorcery and witchcraft.[22] Warwick executed Elizabeth Woodville's father, and he doubtlessly had a plan to get rid of an influential woman. Jacquetta must have known that a woman sentenced for sorcery would meet a tragic end: her former sister-in-law, Eleanor Cobham, Duchess of Gloucester—wife of

---

[20] J. L. Laynesmith, *The Last Medieval Queens*, p. 66.

[21] David Baldwin, *Elizabeth Woodville*, p. 153.
Annette Carson, *Richard III: The Maligned King*

[22] Arlene Okerlund, *Elizabeth, England's Slandered Queen*, p. 113.

Humphrey, Duke of Gloucester, brother of Henry V—was a convicted sorceress imprisoned until the end of her life.

Perhaps Jacquetta witnessed Eleanor's humiliating public penance as she walked barefoot through the streets of London carrying a two-pound lighted candle.[23] The duchess was accused of interfering with her husband's free will and luring him into marriage. She was not entirely without fault though: she admitted to employing two priests who dabbled in the dark arts to cast the King's horoscope in order to find out if her husband would succeed him. She also admitted that she used their help in order to conceive a child. Eventually Eleanor was found guilty, sentenced to life imprisonment and her marriage was dissolved. Her accomplices either died in prison or were executed.[24]

How the accusations of witchcraft come about in Jacquetta Woodville's case? It was shortly after the execution of her husband and son, when King Edward IV was imprisoned in Warwick's estates in the north. One Thomas Wake, the Earl of Warwick's follower, brought a lead image "made like a man of arms . . . broken in the middle and made fast with wire". The figure was allegedly

---

[23] Ibid., p. 114.
[24] David Baldwin, *Elizabeth Woodville*, p. 151.

fashioned to use sorcery and witchcraft. Thomas Wake also claimed that a parish clerk from Northampton, John Daunger, could testify that Jacquetta had fashioned two more images, one representing the King and one representing the Queen, her own daughter.

Luckily for Jacquetta, the Earl of Warwick did not find enough supporters and Edward IV was released from captivity. Neither Thomas Wake nor John Daunger testified against the King's mother-in-law. The men appointed by Edward IV cleared Jacquetta Woodville from slander, and she herself vehemently denied that she dabbled in witchcraft, declaring that she had always believed "in God according to the truth of Holy Church."[25] Jacquetta died two years later in 1472, but that did not stop Richard III from accusing her of witchcraft once again in his first parliament bill in 1484!

Before Richard III officially accused Elizabeth Woodville and her mother of witchcraft, he started preparing the ground. Polydore Vergil recounted that during a council meeting in June 1483, Richard claimed that

---

[25] Cora Louise Scofield, *The Life and Reign of Edward the Fourth*, p. 499.

Elizabeth Woodville used magic to make him feel weak.[26] Thomas More adds more to it, stating that Richard claimed that Elizabeth Woodville had cast a spell on him and had caused his arm to shrivel, although, as More explained, the assembled men knew that the claim was spurious because Richard's arm "was ever such since his birth" and that "the Queen was too wise to go about any such folly."[27]

Melusine

Modern readers will probably remember that Elizabeth Woodville and her mother are depicted as witches in Philippa Gregory's best-selling novel, *The White Queen,* and in a television show based on the novels. Philippa Gregory incorporated the legend of mythical water goddess Melusine into her novel because Elizabeth Woodville was said to have claimed descent from Melusine through her mother, Jacquetta. The tale of Melusine, a mythical creature portrayed in legends and folklore as a serpent or fish from

---

[26] David Baldwin, *Elizabeth Woodville*, p. 152.
[27] Thomas More, *The History of King Richard the Third: A Reading Edition*, p. 56.

the waist down—similar to a mermaid—was known as one of the many "ancestral romances".

The Romance of Melusine, written in 1393 in France, gained astonishing popularity. Written by Jean of Arras, The Romance of Melusine was a work of fiction commissioned to address certain political controversy.[28] This medieval novel became so tremendously successful that it soon appeared in England, Spain and Germany. Jacquetta Woodville owned a copy of The Romance of Melusine,[29] probably because it was an international best-seller and, as historian Nancy Goldstone pointed out, "it was almost impossible for a literate person not to be aware of this book".[30] We do not know, however, if Jacquetta or Elizabeth were especially interested in the legend of Melusine, and as J. L. Laynesmith pointed out, there is no "explicit association between Elizabeth Woodville and her legendary ancestor in surviving documents".[31]

---

[28] Nancy Goldstone, The Maid and the Queen, p. 14.

[29] Luxembourg, Jaquetta de, Duchess of Bedford and Countess Rivers (c.1416–1472), Noblewoman by Lucia Diaz Pascual, Oxford Dictionary of National Biography.
http://www.oxforddnb.com/view/printable/101258

[30] Nancy Goldstone, The Maid and the Queen, p. 14.

[31] J. L. Laynesmith, The Last Medieval Queens, p. 40.

Conclusion

There is no tangible evidence that Elizabeth Woodville or her mother dabbled in the black arts. They were just two women who found themselves in the midst of the political turmoil during the Wars of the Roses. Because Edward IV married Elizabeth Woodville for love in an age when kings were bound by convention to marry for political gains, this match defied ordinary comprehension. The love between the young King and the impoverished widow five years his senior crossed class barriers and upset many nobles of the realm, leading to uproars and the conflict within Edward IV's own family. The fact that Elizabeth Woodville and her mother were accused of witchcraft effectively proves that people could not understand why the King married a woman who, by all contemporary standards, seemed to overreach herself. The sacred nature of kingship made every medieval king God's anointed servant on earth, and the general belief was that kings should not marry for love since love was not a criterion in selecting queens during the Middle Ages.

Elizabeth Woodville was probably a beautiful and intelligent woman who captured Edward IV's attention, and this attraction had nothing to do with sorcery. Witchcraft was a feasible explanation for such an unusual match, and when the Woodville women lost the King's protection, they were an easy target. The accusations of witchcraft levelled against Jacquetta and Elizabeth Woodville were politically motivated—the Earl of Warwick aimed at utter destruction of the Woodville family. He effectively proved that when he murdered the Queen's father and brother in August 1469. Richard III also had a very political motive to bring the charges of witchcraft against Elizabeth Woodville: if the King had been seduced by charms to marry a commoner, then their marriage and all of their children were illegitimate.

A century later, Edward IV's grandson, Henry VIII, would fall in love with Anne Boleyn. Her situation was very similar to that of Elizabeth Woodville: both women resisted the King's advances, both were marked with a parvenu slur by their contemporaries and both were accused of procuring their royal marriages by means of witchcraft, although, contrary to popular belief, Anne Boleyn was not charged with witchcraft during the trial predating her execution. Henry VIII was, however, heard saying that he had committed his marriage to Anne "seduced by witchcraft".[32] The stark contrast between Elizabeth Woodville and Anne Boleyn was that the first was happily married to the King for almost twenty years and bore him many children, including male heirs, while the latter was pursued for seven years and beheaded on trumped up charges of adultery and high treason after failing in producing a desired son, merely three years after the wedding.

Elizabeth Woodville's descent from the mythical water goddess Melusine is a component of many works of historical fiction, and today Elizabeth's reputation tends to be shaped more by fictional than historical accounts of her life. Even some nonfiction authors cannot resist the temptation of incorporating magical elements into their books, feasting upon Elizabeth Woodville's alleged descent from Melusine.[33] Elizabeth Woodville and her mother were not witches, and it is high time to clear their names of slander—once and for all.

---

[32] Suzannah Lipscomb, *1536: The Year that Changed Henry VIII*, p. 69. *Letters and Papers*, X, note 199.

[33] See Jonathan Hughes's theory discussed by J. L. Laynesmith in *The Last Medieval Queens*, p. 40.
Jonathan Hughes, *Arthurian Myths and Alchemy: The Kingship of Edward IV*, p. 110.

4. Elizabeth's reputation: The haughty, vengeful, greedy Queen?

"The Queen sat alone at table on a costly golden chair. The Queen's mother and the King's sister had to stand some distance away. When the Queen spoke with her mother or the King's sister, they knelt down before her until she had drunk water. Not until the first dish was set before the Queen could the Queen's mother and the King's sister be seated. The ladies and maidens and all who served the Queen at table were all of noble birth and had to kneel so long as the Queen was eating. The meal lasted for three hours . . . Everyone was silent and not a word was spoken."[1]

This is a description of a magnificent banquet that took place in March 1466 at the court of Edward IV. It was recorded by two Bohemian visitors: Gabriel Tetzel and Lord Leo Rozmital, the Queen of Bohemia's brother. They were

---

[1] Malcolm Henry Ikin Letts, *The Travels of Leo of Rozmital*, p. 47.

struck with awe at the elaborate ceremony, and today we have a glimpse of this medieval court, vividly brought to life in Tetzel's diary. Unfortunately, this splendid display of wealth and power damaged Elizabeth Woodville's reputation since the ceremony was perceived by later historians as evidence of her haughtiness.

But is this report really evidence of the Queen's aloofness? Was Elizabeth's head "turned by her sudden elevation in rank",[2] as Malcolm Letts, who translated this account, put it? In this chapter, we will take a look at the circumstances of this banquet and examine other accounts which shed more light on Elizabeth Woodville's character.

The banquet Gabriel Teztel observed took place after the Queen's "churching" ceremony. Elizabeth Woodville had given birth to her first child by Edward IV in February 1466, and according to custom, she was considered unclean by society after the birth and was supposed to stay secluded in her private chambers for forty days. Churching was an important ritual symbolising purification, welcoming a woman back to the Church and society and offering thanks for surviving the perils of childbirth. That day in Elizabeth Woodville's life is well

---

[2] Ibid.

documented, thanks to Tetzel's habit of recording his journey in a diary. He reported:

"The Queen left her child-bed that morning and went to church in stately order, accompanied by many priests bearing relics and by many scholars singing and carrying lights. There followed a great company of ladies and maidens from the country and from London, who had been summoned. Then came a great company of trumpeters, pipers and players of stringed instruments. The King's choir followed, forty-two of them, who sang excellently. Then came twenty-four heralds and pursuivants, followed by sixty counts and knights. At last came the Queen escorted by two dukes. Above her was a canopy. Behind her were her mother and maidens and ladies to the number of sixty. Then the Queen heard the singing of an Office, and, having left the church, she returned to her palace in procession as before. Then all who had joined the procession remained to eat. They sat down, women and men, ecclesiastical and lay, each according to rank, and filled four great rooms."[3]

---

[3] Ibid.

Then the guests proceeded to "an unbelievably costly apartment where the Queen was preparing to eat". Lord Rozmital and his attendants were placed in an alcove so that they could observe this "great splendour". The Bohemian visitors were impressed not only with the solemnity of the ceremony itself but also with the huge amounts of exquisite food ("the food which was served to the Queen was most costly"), the respects paid to Elizabeth ("the courtly reverence paid to the Queen . . . was such as I have never seen elsewhere") and the beauty of the Queen's ladies ("nor have I seen such exceedingly beautiful maidens").

King Edward IV made an impression as well: "We saw with what extraordinary reverence the King was treated by his servants. Even mighty counts had to kneel to him . . . The King is a handsome, upstanding man and has the most splendid court that could be found in all Christendom."[4]

The ceremony was indeed lavish and it led historians, such as the aforementioned Malcolm Letts, to assume that Elizabeth Woodville was a haughty queen who forgot about her humble origin. It is true that the banquet was very solemn and hardly a word was spoken during the

---

[4] Ibid., p. 5.

three long hours while the Queen ate. It is also true that Elizabeth's mother "knelt before her", and other ladies of high rank served her on bended knees as well. The occasion, however, called for celebration. Elizabeth Woodville had given birth to her first child by Edward IV, and although it was not the expected male heir, she had survived the labour and the child was Edward IV's first legitimate heir. Elizabeth's isolation from the rest of the court during the banquet—she sat alone at the table—was probably, as Alfred Thomas pointed out, "conforming to queenly tradition".[5] Elizabeth featured so prominently during the banquet because Edward IV wanted to enhance his own regal status and present Elizabeth as the ideal consort and mother of his child.[6] The whole spectacle was most likely staged by Edward IV, who wanted to impress the foreign visitors, and Elizabeth conformed to his expectations, as an obedient wife and Queen would do.

It seems that Elizabeth Woodville knew exactly how to behave in certain circumstances. At the solemn banquet, she was expected to be formal and reserved. But during everyday life at court, she enjoyed entertainment, as

---

[5] Alfred Thomas, *A Blessed Shore: England and Bohemia from Chaucer to Shakespeare*, p. 163.
[6] Ibid., p. 161.

attested by Louis de Gruuthuse, who visited England in 1472. Gruuthuse had sheltered Edward IV while he was in exile in Burgundy, and in September 1472, Edward felt the need to thank him. Gruuthuse was created the Earl of Winchester and lavishly entertained at Edward IV's court.

When Edward IV escorted him to the Queen's chambers, Gruuthuse saw her "playing with her ladies at the morteaulx [a game similar to bowls], and some of her ladies and gentlewomen at the closheys of ivory [ninepins], and dancing. And some at divers other games according."[7] This vividly described scene reveals that Elizabeth Woodville was not a pompous queen who expected people to bend their knees before her all the time. Quite the contrary: this rare glimpse into her everyday life reveals her as a woman who enjoyed entertainment and shared it with her ladies.

The Queen of vengance?

Unfortunately, it has become fashionable to portray Elizabeth Woodville as a haughty queen. Paul Murray Kendall, Richard III's modern apologist, wrote: "the Queen,

---

[7] Arlene Okerlund, *Elizabeth: England's Slandered Queen*, p. 136.

beautiful and rapacious, would know how to show her haughtiness to the undersized lad from Yorkshire with the awkward torso and solemn face."[8] This passage sounds as if taken from a historical novel but, unfortunately, it is taken from a nonfiction biography of Richard III.

There is no evidence that suggests that there was some kind of animosity between Elizabeth Woodville and Richard, Duke of Gloucester, prior to 1483. It seems tempting to imagine that there was tension between the two based on what happened during the fateful spring of 1483, but there is little evidence to suggest such a state of matters. Dominic Mancini, the contemporary Italian observer, noted that Elizabeth Woodville was responsible for the Duke of Clarence's execution and Richard, knowing this, "was so overcome with grief for his brother that he could not dissimulate so well, but that he was overheard to say that he would one day avenge his brother's death".[9]

If Elizabeth was indeed involved in Clarence's death, then Richard vowed to take his revenge on her. Why would Elizabeth want to get rid of Clarence? According to Mancini, "she concluded that her offspring by the King would never

---

[8] Paul Murray Kendall, *Richard the Third*, p. 53.
[9] Sarah Gristwood, *Blood Sisters*, p. 155.

come to the throne unless the Duke of Clarence were removed; and of this she easily persuaded the King."[10] The Duke of Clarence was responsible for the unlawful executions of her beloved father and brother. Clarence also spread "calumnies" about Elizabeth saying that "according to established usage, she was not the legitimate wife of the King".[11] Thomas More certainly knew something about this when he wrote that Elizabeth "highly maligned the king's kindred".[12]

The Queen can hardly be blamed for her suspicions or dislike towards Clarence, but it is hard to believe that Edward IV would execute his own brother only to please the woman he loved. It is more probable that Edward IV had grave reasons to act against Clarence, who was found guilty of high treason. Perhaps Elizabeth approved of Edward IV's decision, but we should not forget that Clarence rebelled against Edward IV twice, proving his treacherous nature, and participated in the unlawful executions of Elizabeth's relatives. The downfall of the Duke of Clarence remains a mystery because there are a lot of unanswered questions and the evidence is scant, but placing the blame squarely at

---

[10] Mancini, *The Usurpation of Richard the Third*, p. 63.
[11] Ibid.
[12] Sarah Gristwood, *Blood Sisters*, p. 155.

Elizabeth Woodville's feet is unfair. Simply because she had her reasons to dislike Clarence does not mean she stood behind his execution.

The greedy Queen?

One curious detail from Dominic Mancini's book damaged the reputation of Elizabeth Woodville and her entire family beyond repair. Mancini stated that after Edward IV's death, when news about Richard III's seizure of her son reached Elizabeth Woodville's ear, she fled with her remaining family to the sanctuary. However, she did not go empty-handed: "it was commonly believed that the late King's treasure, which he had taken such pains to gather, was divided between the Queen, the marquess [Elizabeth's son from her first marriage], and Edward [one of the Woodville brothers]."[13]

This single contemporary source shaped Elizabeth Woodville's reputation for centuries and contributed to her unjust condemnation. Although Dominic Mancini's book is a valuable source of information about the crucial events of

---

[13] Mancini, *The Usurpation of Richard III,* p. 81.

1483, he often repeated hearsay: "it was commonly believed", he wrote when describing this particular event. Mancini's report indicates that Edward IV's treasure was filled with cash reserves, but this is not entirely true.

Rosemary Horrox, who examined Edward IV's financial memoranda, noticed that the royal treasury had been depleted, mainly due to the Scottish campaigns of 1480-82, which were expensive and had brought continual expenditure on defence.[14] There is no evidence that Elizabeth Woodville divided the royal treasury between the members of her family; Richard III never gave orders for Elizabeth to give the stolen treasures back and he certainly would have if the Woodvilles had indeed plundered the royal treasury.

Conclusion

During her lifetime, Elizabeth Woodville was perceived as a greedy commoner who promoted the interests of her large clan using the King as a tool in order to

---

[14] Rosemary Horrox, Financial Memoranda of the Reign of Edward IV, Camden Miscellany, vol. xxix, 1987.

increase her family's wealth and influence. The English nobility, so sensitive about noble birth, perceived Elizabeth as a ruthless upstart who seduced Edward IV and exerted a negative influence on him. There is no doubt that Elizabeth Woodville indeed promoted her family's interests. The clandestine marriage to the King of England saved her from the perspective of penurious widowhood and placed her in the middle of courtly life. Can we blame this woman for using her position to help her relatives?

It is worthy to note that Elizabeth Woodville was neither the first nor the last Queen of England accused of greed or overreaching ambition. Queen Eleanor of Provence was accused of nepotism and greed because she favoured her mother's family, the Savoyards, who flocked to England after her marriage to Henry III.[15] Elizabeth Woodville's promotion of her family sparked jealousy among the English nobility, even though ambition for one's family was expected of everyone during the Middle Ages. She was— and still is—perceived as a ruthless seductress, though it is hard to blame her for accepting such a splendid match when it was offered to her. It is also easy to see why she did choose to elevate her family; as an English-born Queen of

---

[15] Elizabeth Norton, *She Wolves: The Notorious Queens of England*, p. 112.

lowly status, she became a target for the anger of the nobility who detested her on the account of her humble origin. By elevating her family, she sought to surround herself with those whom she could trust.

While accusations of greed are often levelled against Elizabeth Woodville, it is often omitted that she was not as extravagant in spending money as her predecessor, Marguerite of Anjou. The household accounts of Elizabeth Woodville for 1466-67 reveal that the Queen ended the year in profit—unlike Marguerite, who had had a deficit.[16] Elizabeth also reduced the number of her household staff from 120 to 100 and paid smaller wages to her principal ladies-in-waiting. The change was significant since Marguerite had paid £40 while Elizabeth paid only £20.[17] The new Queen cut costs whenever she could – she had five ladies-in-waiting in constant attendance while Marguerite had ten, and she employed one man as a clerk of the signet and secretary.[18] Elizabeth Woodville's previous experience as a wife and household manager certainly taught her a good deal of thriftiness.

---

[16] Arlene Okerlund, *Elizabeth: England's Slandered Queen*, p. 70.
[17] Ibid.
[18] Ibid.

It is fair to say that every other Englishwoman put in Elizabeth Woodville's shoes would have met with similar attacks. A King of England had not married a woman from among the ranks of his realm's nobility since the eleventh century, so Edward IV's choice of bride was both unexpected and shocking.[19] Because Elizabeth was an Englishwoman, she had no foreign relatives who could help her if she needed them to. The only thing she could do was promote her own family and fulfil her queenly duty, which she did, bearing Edward IV several children, although their sons never came to the throne due to Richard III's usurpation.

The question that begs to be asked is, what would Elizabeth Woodville have done if she had been able to predict the turbulent life of love and loss she experienced by Edward IV's side? No one could have predicted that this impoverished widow from Grafton would become Queen of England. Elizabeth Woodville's marriage to Edward IV set a precedent that would be followed by the couple's illustrious grandson, Henry VIII. The only difference is that Henry VIII set his foreign bride aside to marry Anne Boleyn, a maid-of-honour to his queen. But that's an entirely different story.

---

[19] J.L. Laynesmith, *The Last Medieval Queens*, p. 58.

5. Elizabeth, the Princes in the Tower and Richard III

Imagine the situation: two royal princes and heirs to the throne are locked up in the impregnable Tower of London while their uncle declares them illegitimate and unable to inherit their father's throne. The said uncle assumes the throne, and the princes, reduced to the position of bastards, vanish into thin air. Rumours start to spread that the boys were put to death, probably by the uncle who wrested the crown from the elder prince, thus becoming King.

In the meantime, the princes' mother, the former Queen, lingers in sanctuary with her young daughters, knowing that her husband's brother probably killed her two sons and certainly ordered the executions of her brother and her son from her first marriage. Nevertheless, after ten months of living within the walls of sanctuary, she strikes a deal with this man and, together with her daughters, is allowed to leave the sanctuary without fear of losing their lives.

The princes in this scenario are Edward IV's sons, who mysteriously disappeared after the summer of 1483. The uncle who assumed (some would even say "usurped") the throne is Richard III, and the Queen who decided to come to terms with Richard is none other than Elizabeth Woodville. As we have learned from the previous chapters, Elizabeth and her five daughters entered the sanctuary as soon as she found out that her son, Edward V, had been intercepted by Richard of Gloucester on his way to London in May 1483. They boy was sent to the Tower, and Elizabeth was persuaded by Richard's advisers to surrender her second son, the Duke of York. With two boys imprisoned, Richard of Gloucester made his intentions luminously clear and laid out his own claim to the throne, hinged on the assumption that Edward IV married Elizabeth Woodville while being pre-contracted to Lady Eleanor Butler. One contemporary observer even noted that Richard "so corrupted preachers of the divine word that in their sermons to the people they did not blush to say . . . that the progeny of King Edward should be instantly eradicated, for neither had he been a legitimate king, nor could his issue be so. Edward, said they, was conceived in adultery ... ".[1] The alleged illegitimacy of Edward IV was dropped and the bill spelling out Richard III's claim to the throne mentions only the pre-contract issue.

Richard of Gloucester was crowned as Richard III on 6 July 1483 while Elizabeth Woodville remained in the sanctuary and her sons within the Tower of London. An attempt was made to rescue the princes, but it did not work and the princes' fate remains a mystery. The common assumption is that they were killed, probably on Richard III's orders. According to contemporary Dominic Mancini, they were seen "more rarely behind the bars and windows of the Tower, until at length they ceased to appear altogether".[2]

The main suspect in the case of the disappearance of the princes is Richard III, who had the greatest motive and opportunity to get rid of the unwanted claimants to the throne. The common gossip in England blamed Richard for obvious reason: the boys vanished while under Richard's custody, and whatever happened to them, happened on his watch. It was also Richard who had intercepted Edward V on his way to the capital and implored Elizabeth Woodville to

---

[1] Dominic Mancini, *The Usurpation of Richard the Third*, p. 95.
[2] Ibid., p. 70.

surrender the second prince. Why was he so eager to have the boys together in one place? Of course, the plausible explanation is that he wanted to separate the boys from their maternal relatives, who wielded the most influence over them. The Woodvilles were never popular during Edward IV's reign and, as Mancini mentioned in his account, many people wanted to see "that the youthful sovereign should be with his paternal uncle than with his maternal uncles and uterine brothers".[3]

Richard III's guilt was further enhanced by Polydore Vergil and Thomas More. Thomas More's *The Tragedy of Richard III* popularised the tale of two princes smothered in their bed by James Tyrell, Richard III's Master of the Horse, with the help of Miles Forest and John Dighton. The princes' bodies were then buried at the foot of the staircase in the Tower of London. The discovery of some bones found in 1674 within the White Tower adds some credibility to More's account, although the discovery is disputed today.[4] The confession of James Tyrell is another point that theoretically confirms Richard III's guilt, but it appears only

[3] Mancini, *The Usurpation of Richard III*, p. 79.
[4] David Baldwin, *Richard III*, p. 116.

in More's account, and the circumstances of this confession are still called into question by modern historians.[5]

To add more mystery to the disappearance of the Princes in the Tower, not all contemporary sources are unanimous in pointing the accusatory finger at Richard III. A document preserved among the Ashmole manuscripts in Bodleian Library states that Richard III killed the boys "at the prompting of the Duke of Buckingham, as it is said".[6] Another document states that the princes were put to death by the Duke of Buckingham's "vise", which means, more or less, by his advice.[7] Could it be that it was Richard's erstwhile supporter, who had helped him to the throne, who played his part in whatever happened to the Princes in the Tower?

In *Whodunit: The Suspects in the Case,* Helen Maurer presented several suspects and the arguments pro and against each one's guilt.[8] In Maurer's opinion, the princes were killed on the orders of Margaret Beaufort, mother of the Lancastrian claimant to the throne, Henry VII.

---

[5] Sarah Gristwood, *Blood Sisters*, p. 375.
[6] David Baldwin, *Richard III*, p. 115.
[7] Ibid.
[8] Helen Maurer, *Whodunit: The Suspects in the Case*, http://www.r3.org/bookcase/whodunit.html

Margaret's involvement in this case is further discussed in chapter eight.

In October 1483, "Buckingham's rebellion" broke out in the south of England. Why Richard III's supporter and friend turned against him remains yet another mystery. Those who favour the notion that Buckingham killed the Princes in the Tower believe that he aimed at the throne himself, while some also believe that he was convinced by Margaret Beaufort and/or the Bishop Morton to support Henry Tudor's claim.[9]

Whatever the reason, Elizabeth Woodville's movements around that time reveal how she felt about Richard III, and perhaps, what she knew about the disappearance of her royal sons. Elizabeth's son from her first marriage, the Marquess of Dorset, managed to escape from the sanctuary and support the rebellion. Elizabeth's brothers, Richard and Bishop Lionel Woodville, also supported this uprising.[10] Elizabeth herself, although lodged in the cramped sanctuary with her five daughters, found the means to secretly exchange messages with Margaret Beaufort, Henry Tudor's mother.

---

[9] Elizabeth Norton, *Margaret Beaufort*, p. 118.
[10] David Baldwin, *Elizabeth Woodville*, p. 102.

Elizabeth and Margaret knew each other well since Margaret had been a member of the court for years, and had attended Elizabeth at the reburial of Richard, the Duke of York, in 1476, as well as carried the royal infant at the christening of Elizabeth's youngest daughter, Bridget, in 1480. In the autumn of 1483, they communicated through the Welsh physician who attended both Margaret and Elizabeth and carried secret messages for them.[11] The two women agreed that their children, Margaret's son, Henry Tudor, and Elizabeth's daughter, Elizabeth of York, would marry when Henry claimed the throne.

Now, why would Elizabeth Woodville agree to support Henry Tudor's claim? This may indicate that Elizabeth knew that her two sons, the Princes in the Tower, had already been put to death "by some unknown manner of violent destruction",[12] as reported in the contemporary *Crowland Chronicle*.

The rebellion, however, failed and the Duke of Buckingham was executed in the marketplace at Salisbury on 2 November 1483.[13] Elizabeth Woodville's co-

---

[11] Ibid.

[12] Ann Wroe, *Perkin: a story of deception*, p. 71.
[13] David Baldwin, *Elizabeth Woodville*, p. 103.

conspirator, Margaret Beaufort, was stripped of her properties and put under house arrest. Elizabeth's situation was far more dangerous since she, her son and brothers were implicated in the rebellion, and she could not hide anywhere but in the cramped sanctuary. The sanctuary was under siege, and the monks were slowly getting tired of their royal guests since they wanted to show their loyalty to the new King. Although it was highly unlikely that Richard III would violate the sanctuary, it seems that he was eager to come to terms with his brother's widow. But Elizabeth was not easily persuaded: the fact that it took a great deal of "frequent entreaties . . . as well as threats"[14] to make her leave the sanctuary, implies that she was faced with a moral dilemma.

On the one hand, she was destitute, stripped of her dower lands and income,[15] her marriage to Edward IV had been officially deemed as invalid and all of their children proclaimed bastards. On top of that, the two male heirs to the throne, her precious sons, were probably dead. On the other hand, however, she had five daughters with her in the sanctuary. The girls, of whom the youngest was merely

---

[14] *The Crowland Chronicle*, part 8, July 1483-March 1485 http://newr3.dreamhosters.com/?page_id=522
[15] David Baldwin, *Elizabeth Woodville*, p. 103.

three and the eldest seventeen, were brought up at court in expectation of brilliant matches and luxurious life. Elizabeth had their well-being in mind when she was carefully weighing the pros and cons of her decision. What could she do?

Elizabeth Woodville had decided to leave the sanctuary, although not without assurance from Richard III that her daughters would be "in surety of their lives"[16] if they came out. The oath was solemnly sworn by Richard III on 1 March 1484 and included a promise that the girls would not be imprisoned "within the Tower of London or other prison" but would be "in honest places of good name and fame" and would marry "gentlemen born".[17] The oath was sworn on holy relics, before the lords spiritual and temporal and the Mayor and aldermen of London.

Paul Murray Kendall, Richard III's modern apologist, assumed that Elizabeth Woodville came to terms with Richard III because she believed he was not guilty of murdering her sons. This notion is flawed, however, since Elizabeth knew that Richard III ordered the executions of her brother Anthony and her son, Richard Grey. If she believed

---

[16] Elizabeth Norton, *Margaret Beaufort*, p. 127.
[17] Ibid.

Richard III was innocent of killing her two sons, why did she hesitate for so long before she finally made a decision to leave the sanctuary? If she believed Richard was innocent of the crime, why did she extract a rather telling oath that her daughters would not suffer death or imprisonment? The most reasonable explanation is that Elizabeth Woodville, knowing that her daughters had no future in sanctuary, decided to set her personal grievances aside and let bygones be bygones, however painful it was for her personally.

PART TWO:

Margaret Beaufort

6. The richest heiress in England

Margaret Beaufort was born on 31 May 1443 at Bletsoe to John Beaufort, the Duke of Somerset, and Margaret Beauchamp. Margaret's grandfather, John Beaufort, the first Earl of Somerset, had been one of John of Gaunt's sons by his long-time mistress, Katherine Swynford (John of Gaunt was Edward III's son). The couple had four children in total, and all of them were given the surname Beaufort after the name of John of Gaunt's continental lands.

In 1396, John married Katherine Swynford, although "there was much marvel both in England and in France, for she was but of base lineage, in regard to the two other wives".[1] The Beauforts were legitimised by pope, but under English law they were still illegitimate offspring. John of Gaunt loved his children so much that he persuaded his nephew, King Richard II, to legitimise all of his children, in 1397. The Beauforts were legally considered legitimate heirs

---

[1] Elizabeth Norton, *Margaret Beaufort*, p. 11.

of John of Gaunt as if they had been born in lawful wedlock, and the eldest son, John (Margaret's grandfather), was created the first Earl of Somerset. When John of Gaunt's son by his first marriage seized the throne and became King Henry IV, the prominence of the Beauforts increased since they had become the King's half-siblings. Henry IV inserted a clause into the statute of 1397 declaring that, although legitimate in all manners, the Beauforts were unable to inherit the throne.

Margaret's father died about a year after her birth, and according to the *Crowland Chronicle*, he committed suicide ("as it is generally said"[2]). Margaret became the richest heiress in England and a valuable catch on the marriage market. Although Margaret's mother was given custody over her small daughter, King Henry VI granted Margaret's wardship to one of his favourite courtiers, William de la Pole, Earl of Suffolk. Because Margaret was a small child, the King graciously agreed that she could remain with her mother, although according to common practice, she should have been sent to the Earl of Suffolk's household.

---

[2] Ibid., p. 18.

William de la Pole grew to prominence from humble origins and was detested by the nobility of the realm. He enjoyed Henry VI's favour for years, but he ran out of luck by 1450. In order to protect his fragile position, Suffolk arranged a marriage between his eight-year-old son, John, and his ward, six-year-old Margaret. The marriage was not consummated due to the children's young age and was later annulled. In her later life, Margaret referred to her second marriage as if it was her first, never acknowledging John de la Pole as her husband.

This marriage turned out to be William de la Pole's doom since he was accused, among other things, of "presuming and pretending her [Margaret] to be next inheritable to the Crown".[3] King Henry VI had no legitimate siblings, cousins or children of his own who could inherit the crown. That meant that young Margaret Beaufort was a potential claimant to the throne, and Suffolk was accused of planning to put his son on the throne.

Although the peers of the realm demanded Suffolk's execution, Henry VI sentenced him to five years of exile. At the end of April 1450, Suffolk set sail and it seemed that he had escaped from the enemies who craved his blood.

---

[3] Sarah Gristwood, *Blood Sisters*, p. 36.

Unfortunately, the public resentment was so huge that Suffolk was not destined to leave England unharmed. His ship was intercepted and Suffolk was executed with a rusty sword on 2 May 1450.[4]

Margaret Beaufort's wardship reverted to the crown while she was still living with her mother. Everything changed for Margaret in 1453, when she and her mother were summoned to the court. King Henry VI had given Margaret's wardship to his half-brothers, Edmund and Jasper Tudor. They were the King's closest relatives, born out of Queen Dowager Catherine of Valois's secret marriage to the Welsh squire, Owen Tudor.

The King had decided that Edmund Tudor would marry Margaret Beaufort as soon as she reached the marriageable age of twelve. Both Margaret and Edmund were perceived by Henry VI as his potential successors, and merging the two together was his attempt to secure the succession in case of his death. The situation changed significantly when, after eight years of marriage, Queen Marguerite of Anjou gave birth to the couple's first and only son, Edward of Westminster, in October 1453.

---

[4] Ibid., p. 37.

In November 1455, Margaret Beaufort and Edmund Tudor were married. Edmund was about twenty-five years old at the time, Margaret being significantly younger, aged twelve. Although she had reached marriageable age, Margaret was slight and physically undeveloped for her age. In such circumstances, the consummation of the marriage was usually advised to be delayed until the bride reached full physical maturity. Edmund Tudor, however, was aware that once he fathered a child on Margaret, he received a life interest in her estates. The marriage was consummated early on and Margaret fell pregnant during the first half of 1456.

Her husband, however, never even saw his child. In August 1456, he was captured by William Herbert and imprisoned at Carmarthen Castle. He was eventually released but contracted the plague and died on 1 November 1456. Margaret, widowed at the age of thirteen and six months pregnant, found a protector in the person of her brother-in-law, Jasper Tudor.

On 28 January 1457, Margaret Beaufort gave birth to her first and only son. The labour was long and excruciating and Margaret miraculously survived, as her confessor John Fisher would later reminisce: "it seemed a miracle that of so little a personage anyone should have been born at all".[5] If we are to believe in the tale first recorded by a sixteenth-century Welsh chronicler, Margaret was determined to associate her only son with the English throne early on. During the christening ceremony, Margaret's brother-in-law named her son Owen, as a tribute to his still-living father. Margaret, however, was eager to emphasize her son's English inheritance rather than Welsh and forced the bishop to christen her precious baby boy again with a name of the English kings: Henry.[6]

It is traditionally believed that the trauma experienced by Margaret during the birth of her only child damaged her physical health and left her unable to have more children. She remarried twice after her son was born, but neither of her subsequent marriages produced children. Later in her life, she would ensure that her nine-year-old granddaughter, also named Margaret, was not sent to marry the King of Scotland while she was physically undeveloped. The Spanish ambassador reported that Margaret Beaufort and her daughter-in-law, Elizabeth of York, joined their forces together and made sure that Princess Margaret was not sent to Scotland too early because they feared that "the

---

[5] Ibid., p. 56.
[6] Ibid., p. 57.

King of Scots would not wait, but injure her, and endanger her health".[7] It seems that Margaret Beaufort wanted to protect her favourite granddaughter from the perils of too-early childbirth, which she herself experienced as a thirteen-year-old girl.

On 3 January 1457, Margaret Beaufort married her second husband, Henry Stafford. The marriage was arranged a year earlier, soon after the birth of Henry Tudor. Both Margaret and her new husband waited a customary year, during which Margaret mourned the death of her previous husband.

If Margaret was happy in any of her four arranged marriages, then it was certainly her third one. Although Henry Stafford was considerably older than Margaret, there is evidence that the couple shared a warm and close relationship. In his own will, Stafford referred to Margaret as his "beloved wife".[8] The couple often travelled together, which hints that they did not like to part. They also celebrated their wedding anniversaries; on their fourteenth anniversary they feasted on curlew, plover and larks.[9]

---

[7] *Calendar of State Papers*, Spain, Volume 1: 1485-1509 (1862), pp. 167-180, note. 210.
[8] Elizabeth Norton, *Margaret Beaufort*, p. 52.
[9] Desmond Seward, *The Wars of the Roses*, p. 133.

Margaret's in-laws accepted her as their daughter. Henry Stafford's mother lent Margaret some of her own books; such a gesture hints that the relationship between them was very warm.

The political situation in England during Margaret Beaufort's youth was heading towards war. The Lancastrian King Henry VI was unable to govern; the bouts of unknown mental illness which ailed him plunged the country into chaos. Henry VI's queen, Marguerite of Anjou, soon emerged as the real power behind the throne. Unfounded accusations of adultery were soon attached to her name, and her only son, born after eight years of marriage, was said to be a fruit of one of Marguerite's extramarital affairs. "The Queen and her paramours" were accused of ruling the King, who was described as "stupid and out of his mind".[10]

Margaret Beaufort's loyalties lay with the Lancastrian King. She was Henry VI's former sister-in-law and mother of his nephew. Margaret's uncle, Edmund Beaufort, Duke of Somerset (her father's brother, who inherited his title) was a staunch supporter of the royal couple and died fighting for their cause during the First

---

[10] Elizabeth Norton, *Margaret Beaufort*, p. 54.

Battle of St Albans in 1455. During this time, Henry VI was taken into custody by the Duke of York.

Richard, the Duke of York, Edward IV and Richard III's father, believed that he had a right to wear the crown. This idea, however, was not very popular, although York's claim was strong. Henry VI, even if not fully capable of ruling the country, was an anointed King. His bouts of mental illness threatened the stability of the realm, but people were reluctant to see Henry VI deposed. The decision was made that Henry VI would remain King until the end of his life, and that Richard, the Duke of York, would be his heir. This meant that Henry VI's son, Edward of Westminster, was deprived of his royal inheritance.

Queen Marguerite of Anjou was not prepared to tolerate her son's disinheritance. On 31 December 1460, she met the army commanded by the hated Duke of York at Wakefield and won in spectacular style. The Duke of York was killed, his head fixed on a pole and adorned with a paper crown. Marguerite's success, however, was short-lived. The Duke of York's son, Edward, Earl of March, won the battle of Mortimer's Cross in February 1460 and entered London in triumph. He was soon crowned King. Marguerite of Anjou did not back down and met the new King's army in battle at Towton in March. She was defeated, and together with her royal spouse and son, was forced to seek refuge in Scotland.

The political change in England was significant and affected Margaret Beaufort's life. Her husband, Henry Stafford, fought for the defeated Lancastrians at Towton and found himself opposing the new Yorkist King. Stafford's father, the Duke of Buckingham, was killed. Margaret's stepfather, Lord Welles, was also killed, and his loss must have affected Margaret since Lord Welles had been a father figure to her. Margaret's former father-in-law, Owen Tudor, was executed after the defeat at Mortimer's Cross. Margaret's cousins fled abroad, only to return later on.

The man who took care of Margaret when she was pregnant and widowed in 1457, Jasper Tudor, left for Scotland to join his half-brother, Henry VI, and Marguerite of Anjou. As an uncle to Margaret Beaufort's son, Jasper Tudor had held the four-year-old Henry under his wardship since 1458. With the change in the political wind, Henry Tudor became a ward of William Herbert, the man who executed Henry's grandfather, Owen Tudor, and who had taken his father, Edmund, into custody several years earlier.

The years spent in the household of the Herberts were a happy time in Henry's life, and he was later affectionate to the family who raised him. Fortunately for Margaret and her husband, King Edward IV pardoned Henry Stafford for opposing him at Towton. The evidence points out that Margaret and her husband were allowed to visit Henry Tudor in Raglan Castle as he grew up under the care of William Herbert, another sign that the couple adapted well into the new regime and enjoyed the royal favour.[11]

Margaret's relatives, however, were far from basking in the sunshine of royal favour. The feud which started between Edward IV's father, the Duke of York, and Margaret's uncle, the 2nd Duke of Somerset, continued into the new reign. Edward IV was eager to make peace with Henry Beaufort, Margaret's cousin and the son of Edmund Beaufort, who had been killed at the First Battle of St Albans in 1455.

After the Battle of Towton in 1461, Henry Beaufort surrendered and received royal pardon. He was shown a great favour, being admitted to Edward IV's presence and given a prominent role during the summer progress of 1463. Henry Beaufort, however, betrayed Edward IV and rejoined

---

[11] Ibid., p. 73.

Henry VI. He was executed after the Battle of Hexham on 14 May 1464. Henry Beaufort's younger brother, Edmund Beaufort, invested with the title of the 4th Duke of Somerset, became a leader of the exiled Lancastrians.

Despite the fact that Margaret's male relatives were opposing Edward IV, Margaret and her husband enjoyed the King's favour. Edward IV granted to them the manor of Woking, Margaret's favourite residence at the time. Although Edward IV continued to show his good grace to Margaret and her husband, he did not trust Henry Stafford enough to admit him to his close presence. Despite this, Henry and Margaret often visited the court, certainly eager to prove their loyalty, and Stafford attended parliament at least once.[12]

In December 1468, Edward IV was invited to Woking and feasted with Margaret and Henry on pike, wildfowl, lampreys and oysters. The account of this meeting gives us a good glimpse into Margaret Beaufort's taste in clothes; she purchased velvet and Holland cloth for her gown and purple sarcenet for a canopy under which she and her husband feasted with the King.[13]

---

[12] Ibid., p. 80.
[13] Sarah Gristwood, *Blood Sisters*, p. 360.

It seemed that Margaret Beaufort and Henry Stafford were slowly but steadily improving their position in the King's good graces. They were probably aware that the Lancastrian cause was lost; in 1465, King Henry VI was captured, carried to London on horseback and imprisoned within the Tower. The Lancastrians were scattered and defeated. Everything changed again in 1469, when the Earl of Warwick and Duke of Clarence rebelled against Edward IV. The displeasure caused by Edward's marriage to an impoverished widow of humble origins and promotion of her relatives could not have been hidden anymore.

The rebellion had serious ramifications for Margaret Beaufort and her son. William Herbert, Henry Tudor's guardian and Edward IV's staunch supporter, was executed by the Earl of Warwick after the Battle of Edgecote in July 1469. The twelve-year-old Henry found himself at the thick of the fray, rescued by Richard Corbet, a relative of William Herbert's wife. Margaret Beaufort's reaction is unknown, but she must have been terrified to hear what danger her only son found himself in. Her motherly care is seen in her attempt in trying to locate Henry when she sent a party of men to find him. Henry was safe at Weobley in Herefordshire, with Anne Deveraux, William Herbert's widow, taking care of him.[14] Margaret must have been relieved.

Margaret's chief concern was the well-being of her son. After William Herbert's execution, Margaret hoped to recover custody of her only child. She negotiated with the Duke of Clarence, Edward IV's rebellious brother who held Henry Tudor's lands. Unfortunately, Clarence and Warwick were not as popular as they thought they were and they soon released Edward IV from imprisonment. They were reconciled with the King in December 1469, but this arrangement proved to be short-lived. Warwick and Clarence allied themselves with Marguerite of Anjou, who was now residing in France. Although the Lancastrian Queen in exile and the Earl of Warwick were bitter enemies, they sealed the deal with their children's marriage.

In 1470, Edward IV was forced to flee from England to Flanders. His heavily pregnant wife, Elizabeth Woodville, found sanctuary in Westminster, where she gave birth to her first son by Edward. The exiled Lancastrians returned to the country and Warwick restored their lands and titles. Margaret Beaufort must have been overjoyed to see Henry VI restored to the throne. The custody of her son was now

---

[14] Elizabeth Norton, *Margaret Beaufort*, p. 86.

given to Jasper Tudor, who agreed to grant Margaret a temporary custody over Henry. Margaret took her precious boy to meet Henry VI, and spent a week with him and Henry Stafford at Woking, before handing him over to Jasper Tudor.[15]

The restoration of Henry VI was short-lived. Edward IV returned from exile and entered London unopposed in April 1471. He freed his wife from sanctuary and met his infant son for the first time. On 18 April 1471, Edward IV defeated the Earl of Warwick at the Battle of Barnet and managed to reclaim his kingdom.

Margaret Beaufort was terrified when she learned that the Lancastrians had been defeated once more and her own husband was seriously wounded. Although implored by Margaret's cousin to join the Lancastrian army, Henry Stafford had joined Edward IV and found himself on the winning side this time. Marguerite of Anjou landed in England for the last battle she would fight in this war between cousins. On 4 May 1471, her troops were defeated at Tewkesbury, and her only son, Edward of Westminster, was slain, either on the battlefield or by execution

---

[15] Ibid., p. 92.

afterwards. The Lancastrian Queen lost her precious son and all her hopes were now buried.

Margaret Beaufort's cousin, Edmund, the 4th Duke of Somerset, was summarily executed on the battlefield. On 21 May 1471, King Henry VI was quietly murdered within the Tower of London. Although *The Arrival of Edward IV,* more Yorkist in sympathy, says that Henry VI died "of pure displeasure and melancholy"[16] upon hearing the news about the defeat of his armies and his son's death, the timing is too convenient to believe in this version. With all his enemies neutralised, Edward IV began twelve years of uninterrupted rule.

With the death of Henry VI and his heir, Margaret Beaufort's son suddenly became the last male Lancastrian heir standing, and his life was now in danger. Jasper Tudor, Henry's uncle and guardian, took the boy to exile. The next time Margaret would see her son would be fourteen years later, in 1485. The exile of her son was not Margaret Beaufort's only problem; in October 1471, her husband died, probably as a result of extensive wounds he suffered at Barnet. Margaret, who proved herself a loyal Lancastrian during Edward IV's brief exile, was now under suspicion.

---

[16] David Baldwin, *Richard III*, p. 57.

Without a powerful husband to protect her, she was vulnerable.

Margaret, however, was not unprotected for long; within eight months of Henry Stafford's death, she remarried. Her fourth husband was Thomas, Lord Stanley. He was a powerful landowner, widowed and with children of his own, who never wholly committed himself to the Lancastrians or the Yorks. The marriage proved to be a business arrangement which suited both Margaret and Stanley; her new husband protected her lands and offered a place at court, where he served Edward IV. Gradually, Margaret came to prominence under Edward IV's reign and tirelessly worked for her son's rehabilitation. The discussions considering Henry Tudor's marriage to Edward IV's eldest daughter, Elizabeth of York, were set in motion. The King was willing to pardon Henry Tudor and welcome him in England as his son-in-law (a draft pardon still exists today).[17] The plans, however, were thwarted by Edward IV's sudden death in April 1483.

The King's unexpected death ended the relative peace which had reigned in England since 1471. Although he had a successor, Edward IV's sons were never meant to

---

[17] Elizabeth Norton, *Margaret Beaufort*, p. 107.

wear a crown. Richard, Duke of Gloucester, Edward IV's loyal younger brother, sent his nephews to the Tower and claimed the throne for himself and was crowned as Richard III on 6 July 1483. Margaret Beaufort and her husband featured prominently during the coronation: Margaret bore the new Queen's train and Lord Stanley carried the mace before Richard III as he entered Westminster Abbey.[18]

Although Margaret Beaufort made a show of support to the new King, in reality she was already plotting against Richard III. Richard was never overwhelmingly popular; he was a great choice for a Lord Protector, but when he reached for the crown, he did not receive the heartfelt welcome he expected. "When he exhibited himself through the streets of the city [before his coronation]", says contemporary observer, Dominic Mancini, "he was scarcely watched by anybody, rather did they curse him with a fate worthy of his crimes, since no one now doubted at what he was aiming".[19]

In Richard III's unpopularity, Margaret Beaufort saw a chance to bring her beloved son back to England. She started plotting against the King and soon built a network of

---

[18] Ibid., p. 113.
[19] Dominic Mancini, *The usurpation of Richard III*, p. 95.

trusted supporters who had the same goal as she: deposing Richard III.

7. What did Margaret look like?

Most of the portraits tend to show Margaret Beaufort either praying on her knees or holding a missal. She has high cheekbones, heavy-lidded eyes, a long nose, tight mouth and a nun-like gown. You may be surprised to learn that none of those well-known, iconic portraits were painted during Margaret's lifetime. Many of them were painted posthumously, mostly during the sixteenth century. It does not mean, however, that there is no contemporary image of Margaret.

The earliest and therefore the most reliable portrait of Margaret Beaufort is her tomb effigy in Westminster Abbey. Here, she is depicted as an old woman; her head is resting on two cushions with a yale, a mythical creature with large swivelling horns, at Margaret's feet. The effigy was modelled in bronze and was once partly gilded and painted.[1] The effigy was sculpted by the renowned Florentine master,

---

[1] Lady Margaret Hall, *The Brown Book*, A Commemorative Edition for the 500th Anniversary of the Death of Lady Margaret Beaufort, pp. 22, 23.

Piero Torrigiano, but the alternative designs for the tomb were produced by the Dutch painter Meynnart Wewyck, who previously painted "the picture and image of the said lady".[2]

Margaret Beaufort certainly sat for a portrait during her lifetime. Henry VII employed the best European painters and it seems highly possible that he would have the image of his "most dearest mother, Margaret, Countess of Richmond"[3] immortalised. The inventories of the Royal Collection clearly show that the collection once contained a contemporary portrait of Margaret, which was unfortunately lost in the early eighteenth century.[4] The fact that all posthumously painted portraits of Henry VII's mother show her in one of two poses (kneeling in prayer or holding a missal) and in similar dress, points to the possibility that they are all copies or variations of a much earlier image or images.[5]

Although Margaret Beaufort was very religious, the nun-like gown in which she is depicted may be deceiving. Throughout her life, Margaret was a very wealthy woman

---

[2] Ibid., p. 22.
[3] Elizabeth Norton, *Margaret Beaufort*, p. 142.
[4] Lady Margaret Hall, *The Brown Book*, A Commemorative Edition for the 500th Anniversary of the Death of Lady Margaret Beaufort, p. 19.
[5] Ibid., p. 20.

and she enjoyed luxury. Later in her life, she translated a book entitled *The Mirror of Gold*, which contains a warning not to love the world and material things, and Margaret certainly attempted to live by this rule. However, she enjoyed luxury, and accounts of her wardrobe which survived to our times reveal Margaret's personal tastes in clothing. The person of the formidable King's mother can be glimpsed in her gown of velvet, several yards of tawny coloured fabric purchased for a kirtle or her elaborately furred gowns.[6]

Her wardrobe after her death contained seven gowns of black velvet with ermine trim, and black fabric was very expensive due to the large quantity of dye required to produce it.[7] During special courtly occasions, Margaret Beaufort was often dressed in the same manner as her daughter-in-law, Queen Elizabeth of York. The only difference between her and the Queen was that Margaret was never allowed to wear a crown, but she compensated this by wearing a "rich coronal".[8]

The objects which the King's mother used in her daily life were no les elaborate than her clothes; she had

---

[6] Elizabeth Norton, *Margaret Beaufort*, p. 142.
[7] Sarah Gristwood, *Blood Sisters*, p. 334.
[8] Ibid., p. 272.

golden spectacles, combs of ivory, silver pots for medicines, books bound in velvet and a small gilt shrine to hold reliquaries.[9] Perhaps Margaret Beaufort was not as beautiful as Elizabeth Woodville or Elizabeth of York, but she was, however, every inch as queenly as were they.

---

[9] Ibid., p. 333.

8. Margaret Beaufort and the plots of 1483

Before Richard III's coronation, the two sons of Edward IV were put in the Tower of London. Several weeks after the coronation, an attempt was made to rescue the princes by starting fires in London. This plan failed and three men were executed. Interestingly, Margaret Beaufort was linked to this plan: some historians suggested that she was involved in a plan to rescue the princes.[1]

During the summer of 1483, rumours spread that the princes had been murdered. The common opinion pointed an accusatory finger at either Richard III or the Duke of Buckingham. Now, with the two undisputable heirs to the throne removed, Margaret Beaufort saw her chance to bring her beloved son back from exile. The unpopularity of Richard III made the plotting easier, and Margaret probably

---

[1] Elizabeth Norton, *Margaret Beaufort*, p. 114.

realised that her son had as good a claim to the throne as Richard.

In the autumn of 1483, the rebellion broke out in the south of England. Known as "Buckingham's rebellion", it was the first serious movement aimed at deposing Richard III. Although the rebellion bears the name of the Duke of Buckingham, he was not its leader at the time. Why Henry Stafford, the Duke of Buckingham, turned against Richard III remains unknown. He was Richard's staunch supporter and acted as a kingmaker of sorts during the spring of 1483. One plausible theory is that ambitious Buckingham expected more rewards from Richard III and was disappointed when the new King refused to grant him the earldom of Hertford.[2] Another explanation is that Buckingham was persuaded by John Morton, the bishop of Ely (who found himself assigned to Buckingham's custody), to join the rebellion and restore Edward V in order to have more power in the new government.[3] Yet another theory is that Buckingham coveted the crown for himself since he had a good claim to the throne.[4] It also could have been that Buckingham

---

[2] Ibid.
[3] David Baldwin, *Elizabeth Woodville*, p.102.
[4] Elizabeth Norton, *Margaret Beaufort*, p. 116.

learned that Richard III had ordered the murder of the Princes in the Tower and found this crime hard to accept.

Margaret Beaufort remained in contact with the Duke of Buckingham; according to *Hall's Chronicle*, they met by chance before the rebellion on the road between Worcester and Bridgnorth. When Buckingham returned home to Brecon Castle, the bishop of Ely convinced him to join forces with Margaret Beaufort and link his rebellion to Henry Tudor's cause.[5] Margaret's trusted servant, Reginald Bray, acted as messenger between Buckingham and Margaret. Margaret Beaufort was already in contact with Elizabeth Woodville, who was still in sanctuary with her daughters at that time. The two women communicated through the Welsh doctor, Lewis Caerleon, and they made a decision to seal the alliance between them by marrying their children: Henry Tudor would marry Elizabeth of York.

Contemporary sources reveal that Buckingham's rebellion was a separate plot and was joined with a plot developed by Margaret Beaufort and Elizabeth Woodville. Several sources reveal that Margaret Beaufort was the instigator of both conspiracies and, thanks to her wit and political acumen, was able to convince the Duke of

---

[5] Ibid., p. 118.

Buckingham to join her plot. Polydore Vergil stated that Margaret was "commonly called the head of that conspiracy",[6] while the *Crowland Chronicle* reports only that Buckingham agreed to be its leader. The seventeenth-century writer, George Buck, called Margaret Beaufort the "cunning countess" and repeated the earlier assertions that she not only envisaged the two plots, but also combined them into one.[7]

What is clearly visible from the sources is the fact that Elizabeth Woodville joined the conspiracy and allowed her family members (including her eldest son and brothers) to become deeply involved. It is highly possible that the news of her royal sons' deaths reached Elizabeth's ear and she decided to support Henry Tudor's claim to the throne by ensuring that her eldest daughter married him and became Queen consort.

Unfortunately, Buckingham's rebellion failed miserably due to extremely bad weather, the desertion of troops and Richard III's swift action. Henry Tudor, unaware of the rebellion's failure, sailed from Brittany to England, but his fleet was scattered by storms and the coast at Dorset

---

[6] Helen Maurer, *Whodunit: The Suspects in the Case*. Ricardian Register, Summer 1983, 4-27. [available online at www.r3.org]
[7] George Buck, *The History of King Richard the Third*, p. 64.

was guarded with armed men. He was forced to turn around and go back to Brittany, where a group of exiles, including Elizabeth Woodville's eldest son, awaited him. In December 1483, Henry Tudor made a solemn promise at Rennes Cathedral, that he would one day marry Elizabeth of York.

The Duke of Buckingham was executed on 2 November 1483. Before the execution, he begged to have an audience with Richard III, but his pleas were refused. Buckingham's son, Edward Stafford, claimed that his father wanted to stab Richard III with a dagger he carried up his sleeve during the audience. Helen Maurer, on the other hand, suggested that Buckingham intended to beg for forgiveness by making the excuse that it was Margaret Beaufort who convinced him to participate in her conspiracy.[8]

Shortly after the Duke of Buckingham's execution, Richard III shifted his attention to his co-conspirators. The key players involved in the conspiracy had either fled from the country or were hiding in sanctuary. The only person who could be fully punished by the King was Margaret Beaufort. She was attainted for treason and named "mother

---

[8] Helen Maurer, *Whodunit: The Suspects in the Case*. Ricardian Register, Summer 1983, 4-27. [available online at www.r3.org]

to the King's great rebel and traitor"[9] and forbidden to communicate with her son. She was probably saved by her husband's conspicuous show of loyalty to Richard III and avoided execution on that account. Margaret was placed under house arrest and her goods and lands were confiscated and passed to her husband, Thomas Stanley. Her husband, however, allowed Margaret to communicate with Henry Tudor and proved later on that he was eager to promote his stepson's interests.

Margaret Beaufort's actions proved that she was indeed a "politic and subtle lady",[10] as one seventeenth-century writer called her. She was prepared to fight for her son's right to the throne and proved to be a great ally. But just how far was Margaret prepared to go for her son's cause? Aforementioned seventeenth-century writer George Buck claimed to have "read in an old manuscript book . . . that Dr Morton and a certain countess, conspiring the deaths of the sons of King Edward and some other, resolved that these treacheries should be executed by poison and sorcery".[11]

---

[9] Elizabeth Norton, *Margaret Beaufort*, p. 122.
[10] Ibid., p. 118.
[11] Helen Maurer, *Whodunit: The Suspects in the Case*. Ricardian Register, Summer 1983, 4-27. [available online at www.r3.org]

In her article analysing the evidence for the different candidates in the case of the disappearance of the Princes in the Tower, Helen Maurer points out that Margaret Beaufort could have ordered the murder. Maurer argues that Margaret Beaufort was motivated by a mother's fear for her son's life, and she remained in contact with all of the people involved in Buckingham's rebellion. She had both motive and opportunity to pull the right strings and order the princes' murder. However, the major argument against Margaret's guilt is that she was not named by any surviving contemporary source in connection with the princes' deaths.[12] The statement made by George Buck, who claimed to have seen all sorts of "old manuscripts", as we shall see later in the book, is not enough to accept the notion of Margaret's guilt. We should not forget that it was Richard III who imprisoned Edward V and implored Elizabeth Woodville to release her second son from sanctuary in the first place. It seems that the disappearance of the Princes in the Tower will forever remained an unsolved mystery.

---

[12] Ibid.

9. Was Margaret Beaufort a "mother-in-law from hell"?

"Lady Margaret, who enjoyed quasi-Queen Mother status as 'my lady the King's Mother', was a termagant. She was an unlovely mixture of devotee and snob, equally committed to precise religious observance, on the one hand, and to the finest nuances of social punctilio, on the other. She also fancied herself as an expert in household management. She was, in short, the mother-in-law from hell".[1]

This is how historian David Starkey summarised Margaret Beaufort's personality and how Margaret functions in popular imagination. She has a reputation of being a formidable mother-in-law, partly as a result of the great influence she held over her son, and partly as a result of the fact that her daughter-in-law, Elizabeth of York, remains a relatively obscure historical figure. While we

---

[1] David Starkey, *Six Wives: The Queens of Henry VIII*, p. 28.

know that Margaret Beaufort was a strong-willed woman from her early youth, it is harder to evaluate Elizabeth of York's personality. There is evidence which suggests that Elizabeth, as we will see in the next part of this book, was able to be decisive and even feared by her opponents, but she somehow blended into the shadows after she became Queen consort.

Henry VII honoured his promise and married Elizabeth of York on 18 January 1486. As the eldest daughter and heir of Edward IV, Elizabeth was overwhelmingly popular in England. Her Yorkist descent made her the perfect bride for a relatively unknown Henry Tudor, who had spent most of his life in exile. "He is disliked", wrote the Spanish ambassador about Henry VII, "but the Queen is beloved, because she is powerless."[2] The similar opinion was voiced by the sub-prior of Santa Cruz in his letter to Ferdinand of Aragon and Isabella of Castile: "The Queen is a very noble woman, and much beloved. She is kept in subjection by the mother of the King."[3] The advice included at the end of this dispatch is especially interesting: "it would be a good thing to write often to her [Elizabeth of York], and

---

[2] *Calendar of State Papers*, Spain, Volume 1, note 210.
[3] Ibid., note 205.

to show her a little love."[4] At that time Elizabeth of York's firstborn son was engaged to Isabella of Castile's youngest daughter, so the letters between the two countries were frequently exchanged. One would like to ask if Elizabeth of York's role at court was so marginalised that she needed "a little love" from the Spanish royal family!

The picture of the political situation in England during Henry VII's reign that emerges from contemporary accounts depicts Margaret Beaufort as a decisive woman with almost regal status. She worked for her son's aggrandizement behind the scenes during the turbulent years spent in planning his return and later plotting to destroy his enemies. Margaret passed her own right to the throne to her only son and, naturally, she expected to be rewarded. Henry VII, either out of love or sense of obligation, allowed his mother to play a prominent role at court.

"The King is much influenced by his mother and his followers in affairs of personal interest and in others", reported the Spanish ambassador, Pedro de Ayala. Elizabeth of York's feelings about Margaret Beaufort's influence are recorded as well in his dispatch: "The Queen, as is generally

---

[4] Ibid.

the case, does not like it."[5] "As is generally the case" probably refers to his own perception of relations between mothers and daughters-in-law.

To this day, many young women struggle with their formidable mothers-in-law, desperately trying to establish themselves as authority within their own households. Back in the medieval period, however, it was much more complicated than it is today. Margaret Beaufort and Elizabeth of York were born into times where mothers-in-law played huge roles in the lives of their married children. Elizabeth of York's own mother struggled with both of her mothers-in-law; Elizabeth Woodville's dowry lands had been claimed by her first husband's mother, Lady Ferrers; and Edward IV's mother, Cecily Neville, was outraged when she discovered that her son had married a commoner. Margaret Beaufort, on the other hand, experienced a good relationship with one of her three mothers-in-law; Henry Stafford's mother referred to Margaret as her daughter in her will and lent her some valuable books, an indication that they were close.

There is a great deal of evidence that Margaret Beaufort considered herself to have a queenly rank. She had

---

[5] Ibid., note 210.

a claim to the throne, but as a woman, she could not have become the Queen in her own right—the idea of a female monarch was not popular at the time—so she transferred her royal claim to her only son. But she never forgot about her status and emphasized it whenever she had the opportunity. The main room in her favourite residence at Collyweston was suggestively called "the Queen's Chamber".[6] Margaret also adopted the title of "My Lady, the King's mother" and signed her letters and documents as "Margaret R." Before Henry VII became king, Margaret signed her letters as "M. Richmond", her name being traditionally abbreviated and her title (Countess of Richmond) written in full. Soon after Henry's accession, however, Margaret emphasized her royal status; while "Margaret R." could have stood for "Margaret Richmond", it is more probable that it stood for "Margaret Regina", which means "Margaret the Queen".[7]

It seems that the King had nothing against his mother's influence in his private life and at court. At the Palace of Woodstock, Margaret's lodgings were linked to Henry's by a withdrawing chamber, indicating that the two often met in private, and Margaret had used her son's tacit

---

[6] Elizabeth Norton, *Margaret Beaufort*, p. 150.
[7] Ibid., p. 157.

approval in order to exert her power within the royal household. The primary sources reveal that Margaret Beaufort was a woman who enjoyed being in control. She fancied herself as an expert in household management and laid down a strict set of ordinances which set out correct protocol, touching on subjects such as the Queen's confinement, the christening ceremony of the children, arrangements for the royal nursery and even funerals.

Margaret Beaufort was very fond of her grandchildren and took special care that their arrival in the world was always splendid. She drew up a set of ordinances which set out the correct protocol of the lying-in chamber—the Queen's confinement—designating such details as the location and even the number of cushions and types of furnishings and decorations within the Queen's chambers.[8]

One may wonder why Margaret Beaufort decided to draw up all those rules concerning a subject that was probably very painful for her to recall—as we remember from previous chapters, Margaret gave birth to her only son at the age of thirteen and the birth left her damaged and unable to have more children. Perhaps Margaret drew from her own experience; it is possible that she wanted her

---

[8] Ibid., p. 159.

daughter-in-law to have as much comfort and luxury around her as possible—something Margaret probably did not have during her own excruciating labour. It is equally possible that Margaret observed the courtly protocol while she served at court during Edward IV's reign, when Elizabeth Woodville was annually pregnant from the beginning of her marriage until three years before Edward's death.

It is hard to establish what Elizabeth of York thought about Margaret's rules or if she ever tried to rebel against them. In 1489, for instance, she admitted foreign ambassadors to her confinement chamber—a clear breach of the protocol so meticulously established by Margaret, so perhaps Elizabeth of York was able to assert herself against the dominance of her mother-in-law.[9]

Margaret also appeared with the royal couple, often dressed in the same gown as the Queen herself, albeit Margaret never wore a crown—she had a rich coronal instead—and always walked two steps behind Elizabeth of York.[10] Such precautions were necessary since after the coronation, Elizabeth of York outranked her mother-in-law and was the first lady in the land. She was also very popular

---

[9] Ibid., p. 161.
[10] Sarah Gristwood, *Blood Sisters*, p. 272.

because she was very well known to the people of England: she was their princess—while Henry VII was perceived as a stranger.

Behind the scenes, however, it was Margaret Beaufort who was the most important woman in Henry VII's life and she made sure she was in charge of everything. One particular situation described by John Hewick, who petitioned Elizabeth of York, throws some light on the relationship between Margaret Beaufort and her daughter-in-law. Hewick approached the Queen, who listened to his plea and would, most probably, help him since she was renowned for her charitable deeds. Hewick, however, felt that he should have spoken longer to the Queen, but Margaret Beaufort, "that strong whore, the King's mother",[11] intervened and set him aside. This situation reveals that Margaret was very much in charge, and Hewick, perhaps, should have considered petitioning her instead of the Queen. The people of England certainly knew what Hewick learned from his own example—that Margaret Beaufort was a force to be reckoned with. Even the Masses were celebrated "for the good estate of the King, Elizabeth

---

[11] Barbara A. Hanawalt, Kathryn Louise Reyerson, *City and Spectacle in Medieval Europe*, p. 208.

Queen of England, Prince Arthur and the King's mother, the Countess of Richmond, and for their souls after death".[12]

That is not to say, however, that there was some kind of rivalry between Elizabeth of York and Margaret Beaufort. The two women often acted together when it came to the royal children—"our sweet children"[13]—as Margaret called the only grandchildren she would ever have. In 1498, Elizabeth and Margaret both pressed Henry VII to postpone the wedding between the King of Scotland and Princess Margaret because the girl was "so delicate and weak".[14] Princess Margaret, her grandmother's favourite, was only nine years old, and Elizabeth and Margaret feared that "the King of Scots would not wait, but injure her, and endanger her health".[15] Margaret Beaufort certainly wanted her precious granddaughter to avoid the risk of early childbirth she herself had endured at the tender age of thirteen. When he spoke about the match, Henry VII admitted that "the Queen and my mother"[16] were against

---

[12] William Campbell, *Materials for a History of the Reign of Henry VII*, p. 115.

[13] Sarah Gristwood, *Blood Sisters*, p. 272.

[14] *Calendar of State Papers*, Spain, Volume 1, note 210.

[15] Ibid.

[16] Ibid.

it—the two women were mentioned together, as if they acted as one person.

The same togetherness came into play when Elizabeth and Margaret instructed the Spanish ambassador that the Spanish Princess Katherine of Aragon, who was engaged to Elizabeth's oldest son, Arthur Tudor, "should always speak French" with her sister-in-law in order to learn the language since neither Elizabeth of York nor Margaret Beaufort understood Latin or Spanish.[17]

Conclusion

Elizabeth of York is the embodiment of the painful transition between the York and Tudor monarchies, and she is often portrayed as a woman who was trying to find her own place in the new order. Margaret Beaufort, on the other hand, is the embodiment of female strength and perseverance, a woman who knew exactly where she belonged. Thus, the strong Margaret Beaufort easily overshadowed the placid Elizabeth of York, and although theoretically Elizabeth was the most important woman at

---

[17] Ibid., note 203.

court as a crowned Queen consort, it was Margaret Beaufort who was the real force to be reckoned with.

It is highly probable that Henry VII allowed his mother to have such a great deal of influence because while he was living in exile in Brittany, Margaret was working to bring him back to England. Although no letters from that period survive, it is hard to imagine that they did not exchange correspondence. Margaret was probably the only person who truly believed that her son would succeed in becoming King. She tirelessly worked and schemed to see him on the throne, and when Henry finally achieved his goal, he felt compelled to reward his mother.

Margaret was organizing the life at court and even her confessor, John Fisher, remarked on how she often repeated moralizing stories "many a time".[18] It is hard to establish what Elizabeth of York felt about her mother-in-law's constant presence at her shoulder. They often appeared dressed in the same gowns and the only indication of Elizabeth's superiority in rank was the fact that Margaret always walked slightly behind her daughter-in-law in public ceremonials. Did Elizabeth of York resent Margaret Beaufort's influence? Perhaps. But it is equally possible that

---

[18] Thomas Penn, *Winter King*, p. 98.

she enjoyed Margaret's advice and was grateful for her help in organizing the courtly rituals.

Margaret had many attractive qualities; John Fisher, for instance, praised her "singular easiness to be spoken unto" and remarked that she was "of marvellous gentleness unto all folks, but especially unto her own whom she trusted and loved right tenderly".[19] It is certain that the person whom Margaret loved the most was her only son—in letters she referred to him as "my own sweet and most dear King, and all my worldly joy".[20] She loved all of the children born to Henry and Elizabeth and it is possible that she loved Elizabeth as well.

According to contemporary sources, Elizabeth of York and Margaret Beaufort had many things in common: they were both of gentle nature, kind and pious. They both took great care of the royal children and often acted together when it came to their well-being. It is highly likely that the relationship between them was warm and that Elizabeth, who settled quietly into the life of Queen consort, did not resent Margaret Beaufort's influence in her marital and courtly life.

---

[19] Elizabeth Norton, *Margaret Beaufort*, p. 26.
[20] Ibid., p. 225.

PART THREE:

Elizabeth of York

10.The true heiress of the House of York

On 25 December 1483, after Buckingham's rebellion failed and Henry Tudor's hopes for the throne were shattered for the time being, he solemnly swore at the Rennes Cathedral to marry Elizabeth of York. With the Princes in the Tower locked up and probably murdered, Elizabeth, the eldest daughter of King Edward IV, was the heiress of the House of York and a valuable commodity on the marriage market.

Although the rumours of Richard III's plans to marry Elizabeth pinched Henry "to the very stomach,"[1] he was still firm in his decision to marry her. Perhaps, as we will see in the next chapter, Richard III deliberately tried to besmirch Elizabeth of York's reputation so that Henry Tudor would abandon his plans. Whatever other reasons he may have had, Henry Tudor certainly realized he needed to make the popular Elizabeth his Queen because he needed her to attract support for his own cause.

---

[1] Thomas Penn, *Winter King*, p.96.

Elizabeth of York's mother, Elizabeth Woodville, married King Edward IV in an atmosphere of scandal, and while her mother was criticised for her low birth, Elizabeth of York was born a royal princess. She was the first child of Edward IV and her birth was celebrated with great pomp, almost as if she were a male heir. Although declared a bastard by Richard III's parliament, Elizabeth of York was regarded as the true heiress of the House of York. The fate of her brothers, the Princes in the Tower, remained a mystery, and perhaps even Elizabeth and her family did not know exactly what happened to them.

With her brothers, the heirs to the throne dead, Elizabeth was Edward IV's heir. The idea of a woman ruling in her own right was not popular at the time, but whoever married the heiress could have claimed the throne through her. Henry Tudor was well aware that Elizabeth of York's claim to the throne was much stronger than his own. On his mother's side, Henry was related to the Beauforts, a family excluded from the succession since 1397. Henry's father was King Henry VI's half-brother because the Queen Dowager, Catherine of Valois, had married her Welsh servant, Owen Tudor, and begotten children by him. Henry Tudor knew that if he wanted to claim the English throne as a Lancastrian heir, he had to include Elizabeth of York in his plans in order to attract the Yorkists who considered her as the true heiress.

Claiming the right to the throne solely on his own blood was a high risk for Henry Tudor. However, assuming the throne based on Elizabeth's lineage was even more risky since, as Henry's first biographer Francis Bacon noticed, "it lay plain before his eyes, that if he relied upon that title, he could be but a King in courtesy, and have rather a matrimonial than a regal power; the right remaining in his Queen, upon whose decease, either with issue, or without issue, he was to give place and be removed".[2] Thus, Henry Tudor had to avoid all appearances that he claimed the throne through Elizabeth of York's bloodline. In order to emphasize his right to the crown, Henry arranged his own coronation on 30 October 1485. He was crowned before he married Elizabeth of York to show his subjects that he was King in his own right.

In his letter to the pope asking for dispensation to marry Elizabeth—on the account of a fourth degree of consanguinity—Henry praised her "beauty and chastity",[3] tacitly avoiding any reference to her lineage. Henry

---

[2] Francis Bacon, *The Works of Lord Bacon*, p. 732.

[3] J.L. Laynesmith, *The Last Medieval Queens*, p. 59.

explained that although he could have married a foreign bride, he was requested by the lords of the realm to marry Edward IV's eldest daughter.[4] The truth was much more complicated than that: in fact, Henry Tudor was requested to marry Elizabeth of York in order to "unify two bloods"[5] and put an end to the feud between the Yorks and Lancasters. In Francis Bacon's perception, marriage to Elizabeth of York was "most likely to give contentment to the people" since Henry's claim was "condemned by parliament, and generally prejudged in the common opinion of the realm."[6] Henry's claim to the throne was thus a combination of three factors: his marriage to the Yorkist heiress, his own birth and the right of conquest.[7]

Henry married Elizabeth of York on 18 January 1486, five months after he won the Battle of Bosworth and three months after his coronation. The reports from the wedding were lost during the course of history, but it certainly was a grand affair of state, signifying the unity of two warring dynasties. A century later, Francis Bacon wrote about how the marriage was celebrated by the people of England and that people showed more gladness at the wedding than at

---

[4] Ibid.
[5] Sarah Gristwood, *Blood Sisters*, p. 252.
[6] Francis Bacon, *The Works of Lord Bacon*, p. 732.
[7] Ibid.

Henry's coronation—"which the King rather noted than liked".[8] Bacon also remarked that victory at Bosworth gave Henry VII "the knee of his subjects", but his marriage to the immensely popular and beloved by the people Elizabeth of York gave him their hearts.[9]

Elizabeth fell pregnant immediately after the wedding—some historians speculate that the couple started cohabiting together before they married—and their first child was born in September 1486. Henry VII had carefully chosen the place of birth and his son's name: Arthur was born in Winchester, traditionally thought to be the seat of the mythical Camelot, and the little prince's name was not a coincidence either. Henry VII wanted to demonstrate that his dynasty traced back to the legendary King Arthur.

Elizabeth's relatives played a prominent role during the prince's christening. The most prominent of them all was Elizabeth Woodville, the infant's godmother, who carried Arthur Tudor to the high altar and presented him with a cup of gold.[10] Margaret Beaufort laid down the set of ordinances covering the upbringing of her first grandson, taking pride in the planning of the prince's rearing.

---

[8] Sarah Gristwood, *Blood Sisters*, p. 254.
[9] Ibid.
[10] Ibid., p. 256.

Meanwhile, in the weeks following the birth, Elizabeth of York suffered from a mysterious "ague" or fever.[11] She quickly recovered, and a month after the birth, she was traditionally churched and was strong enough to travel with the court to Greenwich.

For a short while, Elizabeth and Henry were able to enjoy their life together and celebrate the birth of their son. In May 1487, however, a new uprising was brewing within. John de la Pole, Edward IV's nephew and Elizabeth of York's cousin, decided to make his own bid for the throne, although he claimed to fight for the cause of Edward of Clarence, the young Earl of Warwick, the son of Edward IV's brother, the Duke of Clarence.[12]

Edward of Clarence, however, was under the custody of the crown in the Tower of London, and the boy who claimed to have been the Earl of Warwick was, in fact, a pretender. Lambert Simnel, however, attracted a large group of supporters who decided to dethrone Henry VII. On 16 June 1487, the King's troops met with the army of John de la Pole in the last battle of the Wars of the Roses.[13] John de la Pole was killed and Lambert Simnel, whom Henry VII

---

[11] Amy Licence, *Elizabeth of York*, p. 135.
[12] Elizabeth Norton, *Margaret Beaufort*, p. 166.
[13] Sarah Gristwood, *Blood Sisters*, p. 260.

perceived as a mere puppet in the hands of political players, was put to work in the royal kitchens. The political ramifications of this rebellion were significant: Henry VII realized, if he had ever been able to forget, that his position on the throne was still weak.

Today we know that the Tudors eventually stayed on the throne for a century, but Henry VII and Elizabeth of York had no such knowledge. During her son's coronation, Margaret Beaufort "wept marvellously",[14] fearing that some kind of disaster may have lurked behind his triumph. Who could blame her? Margaret Beaufort, after all, had witnessed the changes in England and knew that kings were disposable. She had no certainty that her only son would stay on the throne. She probably feared he would die in battle, just like Richard III.

The further realisation of the extremely weak position of the new Tudor sovereign came in July 1488 when the marriage negotiations between England and Spain went on; Henry VII desired his firstborn son to marry the youngest daughter of Isabella of Castile and Ferdinand of Aragon. The "Catholic Rulers", as Isabella and Ferdinand were dubbed by the pope, were cautious: the ambassadors sent from the

---

[14] Thomas Penn, *Winter King*, p. 11.

Spanish court openly complained that it was surprising that Isabella and Ferdinand considered giving their daughter away at all, "bearing in mind what happens every day to the Kings of England".[15]

The rebellion also helped Henry VII to realize that his wife was immensely popular and she had to be crowned. It was an unusual situation since Queens were crowned before the birth of their children, very often shortly after the wedding took place. Perhaps Henry Tudor never planned to crown his wife since he was afraid that he would be perceived as her consort; the recent uprising, however, forced him to act.

At the time of her coronation, Elizabeth of York was twenty-one and still as beautiful as ever. On 24 November 1487, she set out from Greenwich to the Tower of London, wearing a gown of white cloth of gold and damask and a mantle furred with ermines, fastened with gold and silk lace.[16] Her yellow[17] hair hung down her back and her head was adorned with a circlet of gold studded with jewels. She was accompanied, as always, by her formidable mother-in-law, Margaret Beaufort, and other noblewomen.

---

[15] *Calendar of State Papers*, Spain, Volume 1, note 21.
[16] Elizabeth Norton, *Margaret Beaufort*, p. 169.
[17] Sarah Gristwood, *Blood Sisters*, p. 264.

In the Tower, Elizabeth spent a night with Henry, as was customary, and the next day she was crowned in Westminster Abbey. The King and his mother observed Elizabeth as they sat on an elevated stage concealed by lattice and draperies. For Margaret, Elizabeth's coronation meant that now her daughter-in-law outranked her.

The post-coronation banquet was an equally elaborate affair. Elizabeth dined surrounded by the ladies who held a cloth as she ate and sat "under the table . . . on either side of the Queen's feet all the dinner time."[18] Henry VII and his mother again observed Elizabeth from the window at the side.

Although many of the Queen's female relatives were involved in the coronation—her sister, Cecily, for instance, bore her train and attended her during the banquet— Elizabeth's own mother was absent.[19] Why Elizabeth Woodville would miss such a grand occasion as her own daughter's coronation remains unclear. One possible explanation is that she was, as suggested by Polydore Vergil and Francis Bacon, involved in the Lambert Simnel

---

[18] Ibid., 265.
[19] Ibid., p. 266.

rebellion.[20] She could have been ill as well, although the timing—right after the rebellion—seems rather interesting.

Conclusion

Henry VII's decision to marry Elizabeth of York helped to bolster his claim to the throne. Although this relationship was motivated by politics, there is evidence that Henry VII loved Elizabeth of York. You will learn more about the relationship between the royal couple in chapter twelve.

---

[20] Ibid., p. 261.

11.Was Elizabeth Richard III's lover?

On 30 March 1485, only two weeks after the death of his wife, King Richard III, in the presence of the Lord Mayor and citizens of London, publicly denied that he had poisoned Queen Anne Neville and desired to marry his niece, Elizabeth of York. The King "showed his grief and displeasure . . . and said it never came to his thought or mind to marry in such manner wise nor willing or glad of the death of his queen."[1]

The rumours must have been rife if the King had to, humiliatingly, deny them in public. What do we really know about the nature of the relationship between Richard III and his niece? In this chapter, we will analyse all of the evidence regarding this unusual relationship and try to establish what the contemporary sources say.

---

[1] J. R. Lander, *Government and Community: England, 1450-1509*, p. 323.

Elizabeth and Richard

In March 1484, Richard III persuaded his sister-in-law, Elizabeth Woodville, to surrender to his will and come out of sanctuary with her five daughters. The King solemnly swore that his nieces, Elizabeth, Cecily, Anne, Katherine, and Bridget, "shall be in surety of their lives" and that they would not be imprisoned in the "Tower of London or any other prison". Instead, Richard promised, his nieces would be put in "honest places of good name and fame" and that he would make sure each and every one of them would be married to "gentlemen born".[2] The girls and their mother left the sanctuary of Westminster and were well provided for.

In December 1484, Elizabeth of York accompanied Queen Anne Neville during the Christmas festivities and shocked her contemporaries by wearing a gown "similar in colour and design"[3] to the Queen's. The rumours began to spread that Richard III's wife would not live long due to her deteriorating health and that after the Queen's death,

---

[2] Arlene Okerlund, *Elizabeth: England's Slandered Queen*, p. 238.
[3] The Crowland Chronicle,
http://newr3.dreamhosters.com/?page_id=522

Richard III intended to marry his niece. "It was said by many that the King was bent, either on the anticipated death of the Queen taking place, or else, by means of divorce, for which he supposed he had quite sufficient grounds, on contracting a marriage with the said Elizabeth."[4]

Anne Neville "fell extremely sick, and her illness was supposed to have increased still more and more, because the King entirely shunned her bed, declaring that it was by the advice of his physicians that he did so."[5] The mysterious illness afflicting Richard's wife remains unknown, although modern historians suspect that she might have been suffering from tuberculosis and Richard ceased sleeping with her due to the illness's symptoms, such as the dry, hoarse cough or night sweats.[6] Anne Neville's illness was a serious problem for Richard III because their only son, Edward of Middleham, had died earlier that year. The King had no heir to succeed him and this was a politically dangerous situation. According to Edward Hall, who started compiling his chronicle in 1534, Richard "complained to divers noblemen of the realm of the unfortunate sterility

---

[4] Ibid.
[5] Ibid.
[6] John Ashdown-Hill, *The Last Days of Richard III*, p. 18.

and barrenness of his wife".[7] Although Hall was not a contemporary, it is possible that there is a grain of truth in his chronicle. Perhaps, shortly after their son's death, Richard and Anne tried to conceive another child and the King, disappointed with Anne's failure to fall pregnant, contemplated a remarriage.

Anne Neville died on 16 March 1485, on the day when a "great eclipse of the sun took place", and was buried at Westminster "with no less honours than befitted the interment of a Queen".[8] Soon after her death, Richard III expressed his wish to "marry straightaway"[9] and his attention, according to *The Crowland Chronicle*, shifted to Elizabeth of York.[10] The plan of marrying his niece met with opposition and Richard "was obliged, having called a council together, to excuse himself with many words and to assert that such a thing had never once entered his mind."[11]

The King's councillors, however, were not easily pacified and told him "to his face" that if he would not

---

[7] Sarah Gristwood, *Blood Sisters*, p. 229.
[8] The Crowland Chronicle,
http://newr3.dreamhosters.com/?page_id=522
[9] John Ashdown-Hill, *The Last Days of Richard III and the Fate of His DNA*, p. 28.
[10] The Crowland Chronicle,
http://newr3.dreamhosters.com/?page_id=522
[11] Ibid.

publicly deny such rumours, "all the people of the north, in whom he placed the greatest reliance, would rise in rebellion against him, and impute to him the death of the Queen, the daughter and one of the heirs of the Earl of Warwick, through whom he had first gained his present high position; in order that he might, to the extreme abhorrence of the Almighty, gratify an incestuous passion for his said niece."[12] Richard was also lectured by more than twelve Doctors of Divinity, who told him that the pope "could grant no dispensation in the case of such a degree of consanguinity."

Interestingly, the councillors also feared that if Elizabeth of York "should attain the rank of Queen, it might at some time be in her power to avenge upon them the death of her uncle, Earl Anthony, and her brother Richard",[13] executed in June 1483 on the orders of Richard III's newly established regime. Richard III complied and publicly denied that he desired to marry his brother's daughter. *The Crowland Chronicle*, however, acidly noticed that many people supposed that Richard made the said

---

[12] Ibid.
[13] Ibid.

denial "to suit the wishes of those who advised him to that effect, than in conformity with his own."[14]

Elizabeth's feelings towards Richard III

Elizabeth of York's feelings towards her uncle remain unknown. After the King denied his plans to marry her, Elizabeth was sent far away from court in order to quench the rumours. There is, however, one extremely interesting piece of evidence shedding more light upon Elizabeth's feelings towards Richard III. The seventeenth-century author of *The History of the Life and Reign of Richard III*, George Buck, claimed to have seen a letter written by Elizabeth of York to the Duke of Norfolk, Richard III's closest adviser. In the letter, written in February 1484—shortly before Anne Neville's death—Elizabeth expressed her longing to marry Richard III, whom she called "her only joy and maker in this world" and said "that she was his in heart and in thoughts, in body and in all".[15] If that was not damning enough, Elizabeth of York "feared the Queen

---

[14] Ibid.

[15] Sarah Gristwood, *Blood Sisters*, p. 226.

would never die".[16] George Buck, who was the only person who had seen and summarised the letter, attested that he had "seen the autograph of original draft under her own hand".[17]

If the letter is genuine, it gives us a shocking insight into Elizabeth of York's emotional turmoil. But is the letter authentic or did George Buck simply misinterpret it? Did he even see the letter? It seems that he had indeed seen it because he gave a specific source for the letter and did not shy away from including it in his biography of Richard III.[18] Yet there is one significant problem with this letter: the original manuscript of Buck's work was seriously damaged by fire, and the editor, George Buck's great-nephew, added revisions to the original text. The editor filled the gaps and inserted the highly controversial words "body" and "never die", altering the sense and producing a document which potentially damages Elizabeth of York's reputation. In his article for *The Ricardian* journal, Arthur Kincaid transcribed the letter and concluded that "such a reference to a marriage, coupled with mention of the Queen's expected death, along with Crowland and Cornwallis's citing rumours

---

[16] Ibid.
[17] Ibid.
[18] Ibid., p. 370.

that Richard wished to marry again, led Buck to assume the letter alluded to this plan".[19]

Historian John Ashdown-Hill mentioned that Richard III planned a double marriage pact with Portugal: he would have married the Infanta Joana and Elizabeth of York would have married Manuel, Duke of Beja. Perhaps the letter to the Duke of Norfolk was written in order to ask the duke about the progress of the negotiations or to request his help in interceding on her behalf.[20] The letter reproduced in George Buck's book is not, however, the only indication of Elizabeth's feelings towards Richard III. If the inscriptions in two of Elizabeth's manuscripts may offer any clue, we have further evidence of her feelings.

One of the inscriptions is found in *Tristan and Iseult*, a manuscript previously owned by Richard III. Elizabeth of York chose to sign her motto, "without changing, Elizabeth", at the bottom of the page. She was probably the next owner after Richard, although—as Livia Visser Fuchs pointed out— it is impossible to say when and in what circumstances she

---

[19] Arthur Kincaid, *Buck and the Elizabeth of York letter: a Reply to Dr. Hanham*, p. 48.

[20] John Ashdown-Hill, *The Last Days of Richard III and the Fate of His DNA*, p. 32.

obtained this book.[21] The motto is not usually associated with Elizabeth and it leaves us vulnerable to speculations: Did the motto have anything to do with her feelings concerning Richard?

Another inscription is found in Boethius's *The Consolation of Philosophy.* Elizabeth wrote the motto usually associated with Richard III, "loyalty binds me".[22] It is puzzling why she chose a motto with such close ties to her uncle. Was she being sarcastic? Was she declaring her loyalty to Richard? Or, perhaps, loyalty was one of Elizabeth's traits and she simply used the motto she knew well and felt that it defined her personality best? Unfortunately, there is no way of knowing.

Conclusion

The rumours of Richard III poisoning Anne Neville were rife because the King planned to marry Elizabeth of York, or so the rumour had it at the time. It looks like the

---

[21] Livia Visser Fuchs, *Where did Elizabeth of York Find Consolation?*, Ricardian Journal.
[22] Ibid.

whole court knew about Richard's plans, and his councillors forced him into public repudiation of a desire to wed his brother's daughter. Did Richard III really plan to marry his own niece? According to *The Crowland Chronicle*, Richard wanted to establish his kingly power and put an end to Henry Tudor's hopes for the throne by marrying Elizabeth.[23]

Elizabeth of York's feelings about such a marriage are not recorded. George Buck's letter, which came to light in the seventeenth century, cannot be treated as firm evidence since the original manuscript was damaged by fire and the later editor corrupted the text, filling the gaps with controversial words, and the original sense of the letter was, most probably, altered. Today, there is no way of knowing (unless new evidence comes to light) what Elizabeth of York thought about her uncle's advances: Did she welcome them or did she find them unpleasant?

The early Tudor historian, Polydore Vergil, claimed that Richard III nourished plans of marrying Elizabeth and that she "had a singular aversion" to such a match. "She would repeatedly exclaim, saying 'I will not thus be married, but, unhappy creature that I am, will rather suffer all the

---

[23] The Crowland Chronicle,
http://newr3.dreamhosters.com/?page_id=522

torments which St Catherine is said to have endured for the love of Christ than be united with a man who is the enemy of my family".[24] While such a version is certainly plausible, we should not forget that Polydore Vergil was writing under the Tudor sovereign and had to portray Elizabeth of York as a woman without a stain on her reputation.

Even if there was some sort of romantic link between Elizabeth of York and Richard III—and it is almost impossible to determine the nature of this relationship based on existing evidence—would a Tudor historian report it, letting the world know that a mother of future Kings and Queens indulged in an incestuous relationship with her uncle? Whatever happened—or did not happen—between this couple must remain a mystery to us. Today, we can only speculate and the final conclusion regarding the exact nature of the relationship between Richard III and Elizabeth of York is impossible to reach. The answers should be left to one's imagination.

---

[24] Sarah Gristwood, *Blood Sisters*, p. 228.

12. Elizabeth's marriage to Henry Tudor—what was it like?

Medieval highborn women, especially royal princesses, probably never expected dynastic marriages to be love matches. It was certainly every woman's wish to fall in love with her husband, but love was a bonus, and marriage itself was a business transaction. On the marriage market, women were traded as commodities and royal princesses were especially valuable pawns.

As a child, Elizabeth of York was betrothed to the French king's son as a part of the Treaty of Picquigny between Edward IV and Louis XI. The marriage plans came to nothing, and in 1483, Elizabeth's status changed and she was degraded from the position of a royal princess to a royal bastard. In 1484, she briefly became a figure of scandal when the rumours spread at court that Richard III intended to marry her, but in 1485, her fortunes had changed significantly in her favour.

Marriage to Henry VII

What kind of a man did Elizabeth of York see when she cast her eyes at Henry VII for the first time? Despite the fact that in popular imagination Henry VII is often perceived as a miserly, overly suspicious and physically ailing king, that is not how he was perceived by his contemporaries. When he won the Battle of Bosworth Field, he was twenty-eight, some nine years older than Elizabeth. Polydore Vergil described his appearance as "remarkably attractive"; cheerful face, small blue eyes and a sallow complexion.[1] The contemporary portrait adds dark, shoulder-length hair, high cheekbones and thin lips to this description. Henry took pleasure in displaying his wealth to foreign visitors and often wore expensive, magnificent clothes. When the Milanese ambassadors visited the court in 1491, they were impressed with Henry's "wonderful presence" and "most quiet spirit".[2]

---

[1] Derek Baker, *England in the Later Middle Ages*, p. 70.
[2] Thomas Penn, *Winter King*, p. 19.

Henry Tudor was, in short, everything a King should be, and it is possible that Elizabeth of York fell in love with him.

Elizabeth of York's marriage to Henry Tudor was a typically dynastic union. Henry needed Elizabeth to cement his own kingly position, and Elizabeth, who was raised to become a Queen consort, was elevated without the necessity of leaving her homeland. Apart from the political benefits of this marriage, Elizabeth of York was an attractive nineteen-year-old woman with long blonde hair, fair skin and bright eyes. She inherited her good looks from her parents—both Elizabeth Woodville and Edward IV were renowned for their physical beauty in their youth. In 1503, the Italian visitor described Elizabeth of York as "a very handsome woman"[3] although the other foreign ambassador noticed two years previously that "she has much embonpoint and large breasts",[4] suspecting that she might have been pregnant (it turned out she wasn't). Francis Bacon, Henry Tudor's first biographer, who lived in the

---

[3] *Calendar of State Papers Relating to English Affairs in the Archives of Venice*, Volume 1, note 833.

[4] James Gairdner, *Letters and Papers Illustrative of the Reigns of Richard III and Henry VII*, p. 102.

sixteenth century, summarised Elizabeth as "beautiful, gentle and fruitful".[5]

Bacon also claimed that Henry VII was "not a very indulgent husband" due to his aversion to the House of York.[6] While it is true that Henry VII delayed his wife's coronation, which took place only after he was pressed to arrange it, it may be easily explicable by his political agenda rather than his aversion towards Elizabeth of York and her inheritance—he wanted to be perceived as King in his own right rather than a King consort.

Henry VII did not allow Elizabeth to meddle in politics—we do not know if she even wanted to meddle; she might have been as well satisfied with the role of a royal consort and mother of heirs to the throne. "The Queen is beloved, because she is powerless",[7] reported the Spanish ambassador while visiting the court. That is not to say that Henry VII did not use Elizabeth's enormous popularity to his own advantage.

In creating the Tudor rose—a symbol of the two unified dynasties and an icon of the Tudors—the King used

---

[5] Francis Bacon, *The History of the Reign of King Henry VII*, p. 20.
[6] Ibid.
[7] *Calendar of State Papers*, Spain, Volume 1, note 210.

Elizabeth's white rose of York and surrounded it with the outer petals of the red Lancastrian rose.[8] Elizabeth became the embodiment of reconciliation and settled into the traditional role of a medieval queen. She had some sort of influence over the King though: she was, for instance, able to secure the post of bishopric of Worcester to her confessor. Henry had to write an apologetic letter to the pope, who requested that his representative in England was given the said post.[9]

Children

Elizabeth and Henry had seven or possibly eight[10] children together. Their first son and heir to the throne, Arthur, was born in September 1486. Then more children followed: Margaret in 1489, Henry in 1491, Elizabeth in 1492, Mary in 1496 and Edmund in 1499. Some of the royal

---

[8] Arlene Naylor Okerlund, *Elizabeth of York*, p. 53.

[9] Thomas Penn, *Winter King*, p. 99.

[10] Some controversy surrounds the birth of Prince Edward, who died in infancy. Some historians suggest he was born between 1487 and 1488, although the traditionally held belief is that Edward was born between 1499 and 1502.
Amy Licence, *Elizabeth of York*, p. 158.

children died in their early childhood, like Elizabeth, named to honour Elizabeth Woodville, who died at the age of three—the cause of her death was "atrophy".[11] Prince Edmund, whose birth caused "much fear"[12] for Elizabeth of York's life, died within a year of his birth from undisclosed reasons.

When the royal couple's eldest son was engaged to the Spanish princess, Katherine of Aragon, Elizabeth of York made sure to welcome the girl to her new family. She started with writing letters to her. The Spanish ambassador reported that the Queen "was overjoyed"[13] when he gave her the letters from Katherine and her mother, Isabella of Castile. Elizabeth dictated the letters to her Latin secretary, who later confessed to the Spanish ambassador that "he was obliged to write the said letters three or four times, because the Queen had always found some defects in them."[14] In the Spanish ambassador's perception, "the letters were not things of great importance in themselves" but they showed "great and cordial love".[15]

---

[11] Amy Licence, *Elizabeth of York*, p. 158.
[12] *Calendar of State Papers*, Spain, Volume 1, note 239.
[13] *Calendar of State Papers*, Spain, Volume 1, note 221.
[14] Ibid.
[15] Ibid.

When Katherine of Aragon arrived in England in November 1501, the whole country greeted her with joy. She was the first foreign bride in England since the French Marguerite of Anjou, and the people were overjoyed with the prospect of a Spanish Queen consort. For the first time in many years, it seemed that England would have a smooth succession. The wars were officially over and the Tudors were here to stay.

The day before the wedding, on 13 November 1501, Elizabeth of York and Katherine of Aragon met at Baynard's Castle. After a short, formal audience, the two women "passed the season full conveniently", dancing and listening to music.[16] The next day, Katherine of Aragon married Arthur Tudor in a grand, public ceremony. Perhaps the young Katherine of Aragon was influenced by Elizabeth of York and chose a similar motto: "humble and loyal". Elizabeth's motto was "humble and reverent". Katherine and Arthur were sent to Ludlow Castle, a customary seat of the Princes of Wales.

Unfortunately, the royal family's happiness was short-lived. Within five months of the wedding, Prince

---

[16] David Starkey, *Six Wives of Henry VIII*, p. 58.

Arthur died. He suffered from a "pitiful disease"[17] which killed him; he was only fifteen. News of the prince's death reached the palace at Greenwich, where the royal family stayed in April 1502. Because the messenger arrived late at night, the devastating news was given to Henry VII the next morning. The King's first reaction was to send for his wife, so they could "take their painful sorrow together".[18] Elizabeth comforted Henry, telling him that they were "both young enough" and they still had "a fair prince and two fair princesses".[19] Her "good comfort" helped Henry, but when Elizabeth left for her private chambers, she found herself in need of comfort. Henry came in "great haste" and "with true gentle and faithful love soothed her trouble".[20] This scene gives us a rare glimpse into the royal couple's private life: there is no doubt they loved each other and needed each other's company on such a sad day.

---

[17] Thomas Penn, *Winter King*, p. 70.
[18] Agnes Strickland, *Memoirs of the Queens of Henry VIII, and His Mother, Elizabeth of York*, p. 52.
[19] Ibid.
[20] Ibid.

Proof of love

Although Henry Tudor had a reputation for miserliness, he was a man who—although careful with money—knew how to spend it well. His court was filled with musicians, dancers, artists and jesters, so Elizabeth's life with Henry would have been entertaining. The Privy Purse expenses show that the couple regularly exchanged gifts; Henry often presented his wife with elaborate clothes and paid her debts.[21] Elizabeth, in turn, showed him great affection and respect, giving him little tokens of love, such as a helmet garnished with jewels in June 1497 when Henry was planning war with Scotland.[22]

Henry VII was faithful to Elizabeth of York, and that was unusual since the Kings of England often took mistresses, especially when their Queens were pregnant. Elizabeth of York was regularly pregnant, but the contemporary sources do not mention Henry VII having mistresses. The only woman Henry VII was infatuated with was Katherine Gordon, wife of the pretender to the throne, Perkin Warbeck. She was renowned for her beauty, and

---

[21] Amy Licence, *Elizabeth of York*, p. 147.

[22] Sir Nicholas Harris, *Privy Purse Expenses of Elizabeth of York*, p. xci.

contemporaries noticed that Henry VII fell for her charms. She was placed in Elizabeth of York's household, but whether or not she was the royal mistress remains unknown.[23]

Henry's reaction to Elizabeth's death

Shortly after their son's death, Elizabeth of York fell pregnant again. Perhaps the royal couple desired to have one more son, although the "spare heir"—Henry, who would eventually become King—was a lively and healthy child. At the end of January 1503, the Queen travelled by barge to the Tower of London where she "took her chamber" within the royal apartments. On 2 February, she went into a premature labour, only several days after she had entered confinement. Elizabeth of York gave birth to a sickly princess christened Katherine, perhaps to honour the Queen's recently widowed daughter-in-law, Katherine of Aragon. Henry VII awaited the news just outside his wife's apartments and when he learned that his Queen was feverish and slipping in and out of consciousness, he

---

[23] Ann Wroe, *Perkin: A Story of Deception*, p. 265.

immediately sent for medical help.[24] The sudden flurry of activity is recorded in the Privy Purse expenses: the messengers were sent to summon the physician, Dr Hallysworth, but there was little the medic could do.[25] Elizabeth of York succumbed to puerperal (childbed) fever after the birth and died on 11 February 1503, her thirty-seventh birthday. The little princess shortly followed her mother to the grave.

Henry VII plunged into a deep despair. The contemporary manuscript gives us a glimpse into Henry Tudor's inner pain when his wife died. The King "privately departed to a solitary place to pass his sorrows"[26] and let no man disturb him. Before shutting himself away for six weeks, Henry sent a word of comfort to members of the Queen's household, assuring them that they would be taken care of.[27] The loss of his wife and mother of his children was "as heavy and dolorous to the King's Highness as hath been seen or heard of", and the King fell physically ill shortly after retiring from public.[28]

---

[24] Thomas Penn, *Winter King*, p. 95.
[25] Sarah Gristwood, *Blood Sisters*, p. 311.
[26] Ibid., p. 2.
[27] Thomas Penn, *Winter King*, p. 111.
[28] Sarah Gristwood, *Blood Sisters*, p. 311.

Lady Margaret Beaufort tended her son, who eventually recovered, but his life without Elizabeth of York would never be the same again. Later in his life, Henry Tudor would contemplate remarriage—his widowed daughter-in-law from Spain was a possible candidate, although her parents violently protested,[29] and the girl was eventually betrothed to Henry VII's younger son.

Elizabeth of York's body was embalmed immediately after her sudden death. On 22 February 1503, the funeral procession set out from the Tower of London through streets filled with silent crowds to Westminster Abbey, the Queen's final resting place. Lady Margaret Beaufort laid down the set of ordinances for the royal funeral. She, who had planned the details of the Queen's confinement and took care of the rules setting out the rearing of the royal children, now had to plan her daughter-in-law's funeral.

The Queen's lifeless body was carried to Westminster on a hearse drawn by eight horses trapped in black velvet. The wooden effigy modelled on Elizabeth of York's appearance rested above the coffin—the effigy survives to our day and is a fine indication of what the first Tudor Queen looked like. The Queen's ladies followed the

---

[29] Thomas Penn, *Winter King*, p. 113.

funeral cortege, riding on black palfreys. The foreign dignitaries and merchants took part in the grand procession, while the choirs sang and the bells rang.[30]

Conclusion

Although the union between Elizabeth of York and Henry VII started as a political arrangement, it proved to be a happy marriage. Together they had eight children, and for the first time in years, the succession passed smoothly from father to son.

Elizabeth of York's death marked the beginning of Henry VII's obsessive efforts to save his younger son and only heir to the throne from any harm. Prince Henry would eventually become King, and the years spent incubated within the royal household would have an effect on his later life. Henry VIII's relentless pursuit for a male heir stemmed from his father's insecurities, which instilled in him the idea that a monarch must have many sons.

---

[30] Ibid., p. 96.

13. What did Elizabeth of York spend her money on?

The Privy Purse expenses of Elizabeth of York give us a rare glimpse into the Queen's daily activities and shed a little light on her character. Ironically, the expenses record the last year of Elizabeth's life and enable us to peek into her life shortly before her death in February 1503.

The records of Elizabeth of York's expenses reveal that she often moved between royal residences, crossing the river by barge – her Master of the Barge and rowers constantly figure in the records as recipients of payments for transporting the Queen and her ladies-in-waiting from place to place.[1] The accounts also reveal payments to female servants, such as seven maids-of-honour,

---

[1] Sir Nicholas Harris Nicolas, *Privy Purse Expenses of Elizabeth of York*, p. 95.

governesses to the royal princesses, the Queen's laundress and favourite midwife.[2]

The Queen was a woman with a strong sense of family obligation—she gave money for her youngest sister's upkeep in a convent, paid the former servant of her father and rewarded a man who lodged Anthony Woodville, Elizabeth's maternal uncle executed in 1483, in his house shortly before his death.[3] Elizabeth also made payment to the old woman who was the nurse of her younger brother, Edward V, the elder of the Princes in the Tower.[4] Henry and Margaret Courtenay, children of the Queen's sister, Katherine, received financial support, even though their father had been implicated in the Suffolks' rebellion.[5] In the autumn of 1501, Elizabeth employed her half-brother— Edward IV's illegitimate son—as her cupbearer. Elizabeth's son, Henry VIII, would later recollect his uncle as "the gentlest heart living".[6]

---

[2] Agnes Strickland, *Memoirs of the Queens of Henry VIII and His Mother, Elizabeth of York*, p. 54.

[3] Sir Nicholas Harris Nicolas, *Privy Purse Expenses of Elizabeth of York*, p. 78.

[4] Ibid., p. 75.

[5] Ibid., p. 76.

[6] Thomas Penn, *Winter King*, p. 101.

Elizabeth of York was a highly popular Queen and her subjects often brought her small gifts, for which she rewarded them with money. A "poor man" brought her apples and oranges to Richmond Palace,[7] while a "poor woman" presented the Queen with butter and chickens.[8] The Queen also received almond butter from a daughter of the Keeper of Westminster—this was an usual present on Good Friday, when common butter was not permitted.[9] Other presents from grateful citizens who adored their Queen included a carp, puddings, cherries, apples, pears, woodcocks, wild boar, pork, rose water and June roses.[10] Apart from that, Elizabeth of York consumed larks and chickens bought by her private cook.[11]

The Privy Purse expenses of 1502 help us in recreating Elizabeth of York's activities during her last Christmas festivities. The Queen enjoyed music and dances—she rewarded minstrels who played for her and paid a Spanish girl who performed a dance.[12] Elizabeth's

---

[7] Sir Nicholas Harris Nicolas, *Privy Purse Expenses of Elizabeth of York*, p. 4.

[8] Ibid., p. 5.

[9] Ibid., p. 2.

[10] Ibid.

[11] Ibid., p. 78.

[12] Agnes Strickland, *Memoirs of the Queens of Henry VIII., and His Mother, Elizabeth of York*, p. 55.

royal fool, Patch, also received a gift of money, as well as Prince Henry's fool, Goose. Master of the Revels, William Cornish, received payment for setting a carol to music.[13] The Queen also played cards and dice and drank Rhenish wine.[14]

Elizabeth of York apparently possessed a large number of books because she paid for a chest to put books in within her council chamber.[15] The purchase of one unnamed book is recorded in March 1503.[16] From other contemporary sources we know that the Queen owned such popular titles as *Consolation of Philosophy* and *Tristan and Iseult*.[17] She also owned a number of religious texts, one of them known as *The Hours of Elizabeth the Queen,* where she had left her signature.[18] The Privy Purse expenses reveal that the Queen followed the traditional path of medieval piety—her life revolved around religious observations and offerings, pilgrimages and the cult of saints.

---

[13] Ibid.
[14] Sir Nicholas Harris Nicolas, *Privy Purse Expenses of Elizabeth of York*, p. 84.
[15] Ibid., p. 96.
[16] Ibid., p. 98.
[17] Livia Visser Fuchs, *Where did Elizabeth of York Find Consolation?*, Ricardian Journal.
[18] The British Library, Digitised Manuscripts
http://www.bl.uk/manuscripts/FullDisplay.aspx?ref=Add_MS_50001

Elizabeth of York also enjoyed outdoor activities. The purchase of arrows and the ownership of greyhounds tell us that the Queen—as most women of her status—enjoyed hunting. Apart from dogs, she also owned a parrot presented to her at Windsor in July 1502.[19] In the summer of 1502, the clerk of Windsor received a payment for making an "herbour [arbour] in the little park of Windsor for a banquet for the Queen."[20]

The Privy Purse expenses also give us a rare glimpse into Elizabeth of York's wardrobe. Because the Queen's eldest son died in April 1502, she was in mourning and purchased new clothes in black—a gown of black velvet and a cloak of black damask. She wore inexpensive shoes with latten buckles and frugally mended her gowns—one record, for instance, mentions "mending of eight gowns of divers colours belonging to the Queen's grace".[21] She had, however, expensive and regal clothes as well: the record reveals that Elizabeth owned velvet gowns of crimson, blue, russet, purple, black and other colours, and made plans for a gown of crimson satin.[22] The Queen's Page of the Robes was

---

[19] Sir Nicholas Harris Nicolas, *Privy Purse Expenses of Elizabeth of York*, p. 30.
[20] Ibid., p. 31.
[21] Ibid., p. 93.
[22] Ibid., p. 35.

paid for fetching a furred gown of cloth of gold for Elizabeth and orange sarcenet sleeves for her daughter, Margaret.[23] Two years earlier, Henry VII gave his wife £20 to buy gold of Venice for a gown.[24] Among the wardrobe expenses there were also wages for two servants of the Queen's chamber, whose duty was to take care of Elizabeth's jewels.[25]

On 6 August 1502, Elizabeth of York set out from Woodstock to Raglan Castle in Wales, although she fell ill in the beginning of the month. The Queen went without the King, accompanied only by her large retinue. This lengthy journey is astonishing since Elizabeth must have known that she was pregnant for the eighth time. Raglan Castle was a seat of Elizabeth of York's niece, Anne Stafford, and her husband, Walter Herbert. Henry VII had spent his childhood in Raglan Castle, under the tender care of Sir William Herbert, executed in 1469. The reason for Elizabeth's lonely journey is unknown—perhaps she wanted to spend some time away from the court, or perhaps she wanted to visit her relatives.[26]

---

[23] Ibid., p. 34.
[24] Ibid., p. 198.
[25] Ibid., p. 203.
[26] Barrie Williams, "Elizabeth of York's Last Journey", *The Ricardian*, vol. 8, March 1988.

In November 1502, when the Queen was heavily pregnant, she interviewed and rewarded her childbed attendants: one French nurse who visited Elizabeth of York in Baynard's Castle, and another nurse, mistress Harcourt, who conferred with the Queen at Westminster.[27] It seems that Elizabeth politely declined the services of these two women during her final confinement, but she rewarded them for the trouble they took in coming to her. The Queen's confinement was expected to take place at the end of January 1503, and all the necessary preparations were undertaken; Elizabeth ordered a "rich bed"[28]—probably to put in her birthing chamber. The bed was decorated with red and white roses, the curtains were richly embroidered in gold and silk: it was a piece of regal furniture fit for a queen. In December 1502, news of the Queen's pregnancy was known throughout the country since she rewarded a monk who had brought her a gift of "our lady's girdle"[29]—a relic used by pregnant women and thought to ease the pain in childbirth.

That December, the courtly astrologer William Parron prophesied that the Queen would live to the age of

---

[27] Sir Nicholas Harris Nicolas, *Privy Purse Expenses of Elizabeth of York*, p. 62.
[28] Ibid., p. 82.
[29] Ibid., p. 78.

eighty—a wonderful prediction, considering the fact that the imminent childbirth could result in death.

On 26 January 1503, Elizabeth crossed the river by barge and entered her confinement within the royal apartments in the Tower of London. On 2 February, the Feast of Candlemas, she "travailed of a child suddenly".[30] The timing of her confinement suggests that the baby was not expected until the end of February. The Queen died several days later, leaving the royal family shattered. The Tudor humanist, Thomas More, would condemn the "false astrology"[31]—a subtle dig at William Parron's prediction—in a poem dedicated to Queen Elizabeth of York and written shortly after her death.

Conclusion

The record of Privy Purse expenses of Elizabeth of York in the last year of her life allows us to peel back the layers of time and see the woman behind the regal persona. We catch a few intimate glimpses of her—as she

---

[30] Sarah Gristwood, *Blood Sisters*, p. 2.
[31] Thomas Penn, *Winter King*, p. 112.

interviewed her childbed attendants and inspected the newly decorated apartments within the Tower of London, before she walked into her confinement chamber, never to emerge again.

We can see her charitable deeds, attesting to her compassionate nature, and religious offerings telling us that she was a very pious medieval queen. The gifts from poor men and women, albeit small, tell us that she was much loved among her subjects. Her touching care of the members of her family proves that she felt responsible for their future. The woman that emerges from these accounts is religious, compassionate, thrifty and highly popular.

Every now and then, we can catch a glimpse of Elizabeth walking through the gardens of the Greenwich palace— gardens which she herself planned and designed[32]—or hunting within the nearby forest, using the newly purchased arrows. Such intimate glimpses help us to see that behind the façade of her regal persona, there was a real woman—a sister, wife and mother—who emerged as a survivor from one of the bloodiest conflicts in the history of England, and managed to establish her strong position at the new Tudor court.

---

[32] Amy Licence, *Elizabeth of York*, p. 202.

Epilogue: The three survivors and their legacy

Elizabeth Woodville, Margaret Beaufort and Elizabeth of York lived during a very turbulent time in English history. Their paths crossed at various stages of their lives, but it was at the newly established Tudor court that their lives truly interweaved. All of their fortunes changed in the summer of 1485 when Henry VII won the Battle of Bosworth Field and Richard III was killed. Elizabeth Woodville and Margaret Beaufort—who had experienced a great deal of humiliation and pain on the part of Richard III—now, had their own role in creating the new regime.

Back in the autumn of 1483, the two women had struck a deal which came to fruition in early 1486 when Elizabeth's eldest daughter, Elizabeth of York, married Margaret Beaufort's only son, who had won the throne by conquest.

Both Margaret Beaufort and Henry VII were well aware that they needed the Woodvilles, who were perceived as the survivors of the Yorkist regime, to appear at court and play a prominent part in the rising of the new Tudor dynasty. The act of Richard III's parliament declaring Elizabeth Woodville's marriage to Edward IV an incestuous union was repealed, and Elizabeth was restored to her titles and possessions and given the role of godmother during the christening of her first royal grandchild, Arthur Tudor.

Henry VII's uncle, a man who spent years with him in exile, Jasper Tudor, married one of Elizabeth Woodville's sisters, Katherine, the widowed Duchess of Buckingham. The Queen Dowager's family was given a prominent role in the new court.

It seems that Elizabeth Woodville settled well into her new role as the Queen Dowager. Her eldest daughter, Elizabeth of York, was now a Queen and they both must have known that Elizabeth's claim was much better than Henry's. It was, however, Henry VII's mother who was the real force behind the throne.

Margaret Beaufort transmitted her right to the throne to Henry and became his political ally. Margaret's continual efforts helped Henry to become a rival of Richard

III—she never lost hope and did everything she could to bring her son back from exile in glory. Although outranked by Elizabeth Woodville and Elizabeth of York, Margaret Beaufort became the most influential woman at court and suggestively signed her name as "Margaret R." According to contemporary sources, she kept Elizabeth of York under subjection and acted as if she were the Queen herself, regularly attending public ceremonies with the royal couple, often dressed in the same gown as her daughter-in-law.

Francis Bacon, Henry VII's first biographer, suggested that Elizabeth Woodville was displeased at the treatment of her daughter.[1] Because Margaret Beaufort controlled every aspect of Elizabeth of York's life, it is possible that Elizabeth Woodville also resented Margaret's prominence in the newly established regime. According to Bacon, Elizabeth Woodville was "the principal source"[2] of the Lambert Simnel conspiracy. What happened to Elizabeth Woodville afterwards is especially interesting—although she was not punished for her part in the Lambert Simnel rebellion, in early February 1487, Henry VII seized her goods and sent her to Bermondsey Abbey.

---

[1] Elizabeth Norton, *Margaret Beaufort*, p. 165.
[2] Ibid.

Polydore Vergil, the early Tudor historian and propagandist, explained that Elizabeth Woodville was punished because "she had made her peace with King Richard",[3] leaving the sanctuary and surrendering herself and her five daughters. It is noteworthy that the situation mentioned by Vergil occurred in May 1484—why would Henry VII punish Elizabeth for something she did three years earlier? Henry could have punished Elizabeth Woodville shortly after his accession and yet he always treated her with utmost respect and restored her to the dignity she was denied by Richard III, knowing that she had reached an understanding with his predecessor.

It is hard to believe that Elizabeth Woodville would support the rebellion and endanger her daughter's position, but it is equally possible that she felt marginalised at court and sought to improve her position, or perhaps she believed that the impostor was her lost son.

According to Bacon, when Elizabeth Woodville was forced to retire to Bermondsey Abbey, "it was almost thought dangerous to visit her, or to see her."[4] There are, however, suggestions that Elizabeth Woodville was not

---

[3] Arlene Okerlund, *Elizabeth: England's Slandered Queen*, p. 246.

[4] David Baldwin, *Elizabeth Woodville: Mother of the Princes in the Tower*, p. 112.

punished but voluntarily retired from court and remained in Henry VII's good graces. In November 1487, several months after the rebellion, the King made plans for Elizabeth Woodville to marry King James III of Scotland, and it is hardly believable that he would have honoured Elizabeth in this way if she would have been implicated in a treasonous act.[5] Elizabeth was also free to attend the court and emerged from Bermondsey Abbey on occasion.

In November 1489, for instance, she met her kinsman, Francois, Monsieur de Luxembourg, within Elizabeth of York's chambers. At that time, the royal couple was expecting the birth of their second child and Elizabeth Woodville was present at her daughter's side when the baby girl, Margaret, was born. Elizabeth probably resided at court for several months before her granddaughter's birth since the Queen Dowager's presence was recorded in May of that year.[6] However, as historian David Baldwin pointed out, the marriage pact with the Scottish king was discussed earlier and could not be abruptly abandoned, and the Queen Dowager had to meet her kinsman from Luxembourg or else

---

[5] Elizabeth Norton, *Margaret Beaufort*, p. 164.
[6] Rawdon Brown, *Calendar of State Papers and Manuscripts, Relating to English Affairs*, p. 181.

Henry VII would invite suspicion (the King's mother was present at the meeting as well).[7]

The fact that Elizabeth Woodville was absent during the coronation of her daughter in November 1487 may suggest that she was, indeed, punished for something. It is possible that Elizabeth Woodville was implicated in some kind of treasonous activity—whether it was the Lambert Simnel conspiracy or some other dealings, we will probably never know.

Elizabeth Woodville spent the last five years of her life in relative poverty. Her appearance at court in May and November 1489 were the last public appearances she made before her death. The Queen Dowager's health started to deteriorate, and in April 1492, she made her last will. In the document, Elizabeth Woodville remarked that she had "no worldly goods" to bequeath to "the Queen's Grace, my dearest daughter". She expressed her regret that she could not "reward any of my children, according to my heart and mind" and beseeched God to "bless her Grace, with all her noble issue, and with as good heart and mind as is to me possible, I give her Grace my blessing, and all the aforesaid

---

[7] David Baldwin, *Elizabeth Woodville: Mother of the Princes in the Tower*, pp. 114, 115.

my children".[8] Elizabeth Woodville died nearly two months after making her will, on 8 June 1492. She was buried, as she requested, by her husband Edward IV. The funeral was very humble and shocked one of the heralds present during the proceedings; there was only "a low hearse, such as they use for the common people" and "nothing done solemnly"[9] for the Queen Dowager. The humble proceedings, however, honoured what Elizabeth Woodville requested in her will: she wished to be buried "without pompous entering or costly expenses done thereabout."[10]

Elizabeth of York, the eldest child of Elizabeth Woodville and Edward IV, did not attend the funeral since she was about to enter her confinement chamber, but the herald supposed that "she went in blue [the colour of mourning] in likewise as Queen Marguerite, the wife of King Henry VI, went in when her mother the Queen of Sicily died".[11] Among those members of the family present at the Queen Dowager's funeral were three of her daughters— Anne, Katherine and Bridget; her daughter-in-law, the Marchioness of Dorset and her niece; and the Marquess of

---

[8] Arlene Okerlund, *Elizabeth: England's Slandered Queen*, pp. 256, 257.
[9] Ibid., p. 258.
[10] Ibid., p. 257.
[11] Ibid., p. 259.

Dorset, her elder son from her first marriage. The presence of "Mistress Grace, a bastard daughter of King Edward"[12] may suggest that Elizabeth Woodville was a compassionate woman and took care of her husband's illegitimate child.

In stark contrast to Elizabeth Woodville, Margaret Beaufort spent her last years surrounded by luxury and wealth, and she had a great influence on her son's private and political life. From the beginning of Henry VII's reign, Margaret emerged as the real force behind the throne. In 1485, the parliament declared Margaret Beaufort a "femme sole", giving her the right to hold property in her own name and sue in the courts; she was allowed to act as if she were a widow, although her husband was still alive. No other married woman in England was given such a right and it basically meant that Margaret was an independent woman and had complete control over her vast estates and fortune.[13] In early 1499, she undertook a vow of chastity— another unusual step for a married woman since only widows usually vowed their chastity in front of a bishop.

Margaret Beaufort was, in short, an independent landholder and a powerful figure in her own right. She lived

---

[12] Ibid., p. 258.
[13] Elizabeth Norton, *Margaret Beaufort*, p. 148.

long enough to see her only son establish a dynasty that would eventually survive 118 years on the throne, and although Margaret often feared the changeability of Fortune's Wheel, she managed to stand by Henry VII and helped him to create a new regime.

In April 1509, Margaret Beaufort saw her beloved son dying of tuberculosis, but she also saw her grandson—the seventeen-year-old Prince Henry—ascending the throne as Henry VIII. Although Margaret's body started to fail her—she was afraid of losing her sight or the use of her legs—she took an active role in assisting Henry VIII to the throne. The new King's powerful grandmother selected the members of the new council and briefed them on her demands.[14]

Margaret Beaufort watched Henry VIII's coronation procession; the young King and his newly wedded wife, Katherine of Aragon, received a warm welcome and were perceived as a beacon of hope. Both young and in good health, Henry and Katherine were the new royal couple. Although she was unwell, Margaret Beaufort attended the coronation and the banquet and certainly had a sense of fulfilled obligation as she watched Henry VIII.

---

[14] Ibid., p. 211.

Her grandson's coronation was Margaret's last public appearance. She retired to a house within Westminster Abbey, the place she had chosen to die. She was the last senior adult member of the royal family, and her death marked the beginning of Henry VIII's independent rule. Margaret Beaufort survived her husbands, son, daughter-in-law and many members of the Yorkist regime. She saw Kings and Queens at the height of their power and she witnessed their downfalls as well. The sense of uncertainty never left Margaret, and she was well aware that even a crowned King could be deposed. In the end, however, she witnessed her grandson's coronation and died knowing that the second Tudor sovereign had begun his tenure.

Margaret Beaufort and Elizabeth Woodville were undeniably two strong-willed women. It is much harder to establish beyond doubt what kind of a woman Elizabeth of York was. Nancy Lenz Harvey, Elizabeth's 1973 biographer, portrayed her as a strong, determined woman, although the existing evidence does not allow us to draw final conclusions about Elizabeth's character. Not much is known about this Queen's personal character, although her Privy Purse expenses reveal that Elizabeth of York was a compassionate, pious woman with a deep sense of family obligation.

191

There is also a darker side to her character; if we are to believe in George Buck's letter discovered in the seventeenth century, Elizabeth wished to see the ailing Queen Anne Neville dead so her own marriage plans could move forward. The letter's authenticity is, however, questioned, and it is impossible to reach a final conclusion— was Elizabeth of York implicating that she was Richard III's lover when she wrote that "she was his in heart and in thoughts, in body and in all"?[15] Or was she referring to a double Portuguese marriage pact? We will never know.

What we do know about Elizabeth of York is that she was a beloved Queen and her popularity helped Henry VII build the image of his new dynasty. She also took an active role in her children's upbringing—in recent years, Dr David Starkey has suggested that "Elizabeth herself was a first teacher of her daughters and of her second son, Henry",[16] because Henry's handwriting resembled his mother's style of writing.

For Henry VIII, raised in a female household, his mother would always be a paragon of virtue, a woman who gave him a loving and safe childhood. Her death, according

---

[15] Sarah Gristwood, *Blood Sisters*, p. 226.
[16] David Starkey, *Henry VIII: The Mind of a Tyrant*, Channel 4 *documentary*, Part 1: Prince.

to Henry's own words, was a "hateful intelligence",[17] news that devastated him. Elizabeth of York's funeral served as a model for the funeral of Henry VIII's most beloved third wife, Jane Seymour, who also died in childbirth in 1537.[18] None of Henry VIII's six wives apart from Jane received such a magnificent funeral because almost all of them died in disgrace—two of Henry VIII's six marriages ended in his wives' beheading, two marriages were annulled and the last one ended with Henry's own death.

Conclusion

Elizabeth Woodville, Margaret Beaufort and Elizabeth of York were responsible for founding the Tudor dynasty. Both Elizabeth Woodville and Margaret Beaufort were mothers of the first Tudor royal couple and grandmothers to future Kings and Queens of England.

During her fifty-five years of life, Elizabeth Woodville mourned the deaths of her parents, all of her five brothers,

---

[17] Thomas Penn, *Winter King*, p. 111.
[18] Elizabeth Norton, *Jane Seymour: Henry VIII's True Love*, p. 149.

all but one of her seven sisters, two of her daughters, four of her five sons and two husbands.

Margaret Beaufort mourned the deaths of her husbands and the Beaufort cousins—the direct male line went extinct in 1471. She also outlived many of the people who crossed her path during the Wars of the Roses, including four Queens and four Kings—among them her only son, Henry VII.

Elizabeth of York's formative years were shaped by the tumultuous events of the war, but she eventually became the first Tudor Queen. Although she died before her time, she managed to shape her children's early childhood and leave an image of a domestic Queen.

Together, these three women are mothers of the Tudor dynasty. They were survivors who emerged victorious from the Wars of the Roses and found their own peace in the newly established court. Whilst the direct Tudor line died out in 1603, these three women's blood continued in other lines.

Elizabeth Woodville's son from her first marriage, Thomas Grey, the Marquess of Dorset, had seven sons and eight daughters, all of them carrying Elizabeth Woodville's blood in their veins. Dorset's grandson, Elizabeth Woodville's great-grandson, married Frances Brandon and became the father of the ill-fated Jane Grey, England's "Nine Days' Queen".[19]

Margaret Beaufort's and Elizabeth of York's bloodlines did not die out with the direct Tudor line in 1603 either, they continued through the descendants of Princess Margaret Tudor, who married King James IV of Scotland.[20]

Their contribution to posterity is enormous—Henry VIII is one of the most recognizable Kings of England, while Elizabeth I is the first female monarch to prove that a woman could rule successfully in her own right. The Tudor dynasty traces its origin to Elizabeth Woodville, Margaret Beaufort and Elizabeth of York—women, who waged through blood and loss in order to finally emerge as the ultimate survivors of the Wars of the Roses.

---

[19] Arlene Okerlund, *Elizabeth: England's Slandered Queen*, pp. 266.
[20] Elizabeth Norton, *Margaret Beaufort*, p. 218.

Bibliography

Primary sources:

Fabyan, Robert. *The New Chronicles of England and France.* Ed. Henry Ellis. London, Rivington, 1811.

Hall, Edward. *Hall's Chronicle: Containing the History of England, During the Reign of Henry the Fourth, and the Succeeding Monarchs, to the End of the Reign of Henry the 8th, 1548.* Reprint ed., New York: AMS Press, 1965.

Harris, Sir Nicholas, ed. *Privy Purse Expenses of Elizabeth of York: Wardrobe Accounts of Edward IV.* London: W. Pickering, 1830. Reprint ed., New York: Barnes and Noble, 1972.

Mancinus, Dominicus. *The Usurpation of Richard the Third,* Trans. C.A.J. Armstrong. 2nd ed. Oxford, Clarendon Press, 1969.

More, Thomas. *The History of King Richard III and Selections from the English and Latin Poems.* Yale University Press, 1976.

More, Thomas. *The History of King Richard the Third: A Reading Edition.* Indiana University Press, 2005.

Vergil, Polydore. *Anglica Historia of Polydore Vergil, A.D 1485-1537.* The Royal Historical Society, 1950.

Secondary sources:

Baldwin, David. *Elizabeth Woodville: Mother of the Princes in the Tower.* The History Press, 2010.

Baldwin, David. *Richard III.* Amberley Publishing, 2013.

Crawford, Anne. *The Yorkists: The History of a Dynasty.* Hambledon Continuum, 2007.

Gristwood, Sarah. *Blood Sisters: The Women Behind the Wars of the Roses.* Harper Press, 2012.

Kendall, Paul Murray. *Richard the Third.* Doubleday & Co., 1965.

Laynesmith, J.L. *The Last Medieval Queens: English Queenship 1445-1503.* Oxford: Oxford University Press, 2004.

Licence, Amy. *Elizabeth of York: The Forgotten Tudor Queen.* Amberley Publishing, 2013.

Maurer, Helen. *Whodunit: The Suspects in the Case,* Ricardian Register, Summer 1983, 4-27. (Available online at www.r3.org.)

Norton, Elizabeth. *Margaret Beaufort: Mother of the Tudor Dynasty.* Amberley Publishing, 2011.

Okerlund, A. *Elizabeth: England's Slandered Queen.* Gloucestershire, Tempus, 2006.

Ross, Charles. *Edward IV.* London, Eyre Methuen, 1974.

Sutton, Anne F. and Visser-Fuchs, Livia. "A Most Benevolent Queen: Queen Elizabeth Woodville's Reputation, Her Piety and Her Books". *The Ricardian.* 10 (June 1995): 214 – 245.